LOVE TRANCE:

LOVE TRANCE:

Break the Rules and Stay in Love Forever

Dr. John D. Lentz

Copyright 2015 Dr. John D. Lentz
Published by Healing Words Press

All rights reserved. No part of this publication may be reproduced stored in a retrieval system or transmitted, in any form or by any means electronic mechanical, recorded photocopied or otherwise without the prior written permission of both the copyright owner and the above publisher of the book, except by a review who may quote brief passages in a review.

The scanning, uploading, and distribution of this book via the internet or via any other means without the permission of the publisher is illegal and punishable by law. Please purchase only authorized electronic editions and do not participate in or encourage electronic piracy of copyrightable materials. Your support of the authors rights is appreciated.

Printed in the Unlisted states
ISBN 978-0-9836755-7-0
ISBN 10: 0983675570

TABLE OF CONTENTS

Acknowledgments vii

Introduction ix

Chapter 1   You Started Off "In Love" 1

Chapter 2   How Come This Book Can Help 6

Chapter 3   So Then What Happened 14

Chapter 4   When You Were "In Love" You Did it Right 28

Chapter 5   Tips From Your Own Experience of Love 37

Chapter 6   Marital Happiness Research 52

Chapter 7   What Else The Study Said 60

Chapter 8	Spontaneously Thinking Positive Thoughts About Each Other	70
Chapter 9	Doing it Will Be Like Learning to Ride a Bike	80
Chapter 10	Ok, So Now You Have Had a Positive Experience	88
Chapter 11	Keeping it Possible	93
Chapter 12	The Other Side of Forgiveness	103
Chapter 13	Transforming Disagreements Easily	108
Chapter 14	Ways of Generating a Positive Mindset	114
Chapter 15	Coping With Your New Love Prosperity	119

About the Author 123

ACKNOWLEDGMENTS

I would like to thank all the couples who have helped make this book possible by working with me and allowing me to assist them to change their world. The professionals who gave of their time and effort to make comments about the book and then the ones who made comments in support of the book are also greatly appreciated. I also want to thank Kate Hubert MSSW who is also a CSW and who helped edit and make sure the manuscript makes sense. Her comments were invaluable.

Pam Stockard painted the original painting for the cover art. She is a local artist who is known for her work in painting horses, landscapes, and portraits.

My wife also deserves a lot of credit for helping me to understand how to be a better husband.

INTRODUCTION

Once upon a time in a land far far away there was a beautiful princess named Roxanna. She was called Rocky by some because she was so rock solid in her unwavering belief in you if she met you. It was her goodness that was coming out. She was so beautiful because of her ways of thinking and being. She was fair to look at as well but it was her inner beauty that caused people to gasp when they realized how she thought. You see she was willing and able to love you almost as soon as she met you. If she got angry with you it was because you were not treating yourself or others fairly. She was both able to see your good qualities and your not so good qualities and was willing to love you no matter what.

It seems that a wicked Witch was jealous of the Princess and devised a plan to trick her and defeat her positive attitude that made everyone love her. The wicked Witch knew that she couldn't put the spell directly on the Princess because her goodness would see through it and it wouldn't have any negative impact. So the wicked Witch schemed, and found someone who the princess loved and by infecting them with the spell of doubt, to speak up and doubt that anyone could love them as much as the Princess loved everyone. Then the wicked Witch infected more and more people in the Kingdom with fears that turned them into being afraid of not being loved back and looking like a fool if they loved more than whoever they loved. The Witch's plan was working, and so she got even bolder. She infected the Princess's true love the Prince with some doubt as well. Now the witch knew that what she had done would work. It would turn the Princess from being so loving to be hurtful herself.

The wicked Witch was gloating over how well her plan was working. The people around the Princess were beginning to doubt her love of them, and snipping with sharp words when speaking back to the Princess. Oh they would veil their words at first in jokes, humor or just that they were in a bad mood but the words stung. Actually the Princess was hurt deeply because she knew she hadn't done anything to warrant such unkind words. When her darling the Prince also cut her with a sharp remark that left her shocked and hurt because of his betrayal she went into her room and cried.

The Princess cried and felt hurt because she loved her Prince so much. She could take it when everyone else was saying hurtful things at times to her, but when her Prince turned on her she felt defeated. Eventually she cried herself to sleep, and dreamed. In her dream her pillow was a rock and it was difficult to sleep on such a rock but Princess Rocky saw a stairway up to Heaven. On the stairway were Angels going up and coming down and then she heard God say to her that she wasn't alone and that if she allowed herself to be blessed God would bless her with Angels to help. She could sense her awareness of everything around her expanding and growing. She felt good and healed of the hurts. She felt so wonderful knowing that God was going to send and had sent Angels to help her that she rested peacefully the rest of the night.

In the morning she awoke with a plan. She was going to adopt the feeling she had when God spoke to her last evening. She was going to feel that feeling in the presence of the hurtful things said to her. It was like she was guided by Angels because as soon as she was at breakfast the next morning she had an opportunity to put into practice what she had learned. She did, and to her astonishment it worked. Not only was she protected and didn't feel hurt but the servant responded to her differently and with warmth and kindness. So she was encouraged to try it out on her Prince. When he came near he criticized her for running off and barricading herself in her room away from him and the rest of the Kingdom. She grabbed her chest and could feel the hurt and then she could feel the positive feeling returning from the night before. She responded out of her love of him and at first he bristled not believing her, and then little by little he too came around and started treating the Princess the way he had before.

The Princess taught the Prince by example how to transform even hurtful things said to become a bridge to closeness. Together they made a pact to promote their love even without ever saying so. You see they just silently agreed to go back to treating each other the way they always had. It worked and soon everyone in the land was doing it as well and the wicked Witch's plan had failed.

Actually, in the end the wicked Witch's plan didn't fail. The wicked Witch wanted to be loved too and soon began to feel that love because she had done everything to block it and test it, so she just began to believe it, and live it as well. The wicked Witch became a Loving Queen in a nearby Kingdom and taught her subjects all the wisdom she had learned.

This book is written in an unconventional way. It is written to the creative part of your brain. So it is designed to say things on more than one level, and in different ways. Your conscious mind may notice changes in tense, or other grammatical irregularities, but your creative part will recognize that what was really implied was positive and helpful. It isn't supposed to be as logical and make sense as other books, because it is supposed to invite you to make use of strengths that you may not know you have. It is also to invite you to have rewarding epiphanies about yourself, your partner and your future. If the devices that are used in this book also help you to have better relationships with others and family members then so much the better, but only in safe ways.

The different way this book has been written may arouse your curiosity, as such you may notice odd placements of items, and non logical ways of approaching subjects. This isn't a feel good book, or one that appeals to the logical part of your brain, even if it is written so that you will more spontaneously begin to feel better. It is written the way we live, every day with multiple concepts, emotional experiences and facts that alter how we think and feel.

It was also written to a specific group of people. It was written to folks who have grown up with a Judeo-Christian background.

It has been my intention to use shock, or humor, and reverse as many of the negative manipulations the culture did on you that stole some of your ability to be as loving as you can be with your partner. If you get to some place and wonder what is going on or what ways that you are being invited to utilize your strengths, just assume that whatever was said was said for your benefit and was as true as I can know it to be.

You also deserve to realize that I have been as intentional as I possibly could be with the limited dimension of words to give you back something that was your birth right. You were born with the ability to love and be loved. You were born also with the capacity to deeply love and stay safe. I have done my best to give you things that you can alter your beliefs so that you can become more fully loving and be safer than you perhaps ever were before, because it is a mindset. I hope that you allow yourself to receive the positive intentions that are placed here for you to discover and to utilize for your benefit.

Sincerely,

Rev. John D. Lentz D. Min.

"The question of love is one that cannot be evaded. Whether or not you claim to be interested in It, from the moment you are alive you are bound to be concerned with love, because love is not just something that happens to you: It is a certain special way of being alive. Love is, in fact, an intensification of life, completeness, fullness, a wholeness of life." - Thomas Merton

CHAPTER 1
YOU STARTED OFF "IN LOVE"

You started off falling in love. It was a magical time. If you want to get back that feeling again, you want a good thing. It is possible, despite what some say. It is even predictable and something you can do whether your partner knows about your decision to change or not. Well provided that he/she hasn't moved on, or is someone who simply unwilling to be a part of a positive and committed relationship. If you are skeptical that is good. Let's first remember how it was when you were first in Love. You delighted in being in each other's company. It was wonderful and you looked forward to being together each time you were apart because it was so exciting being together.

If we think about God being the source of Love like the Judeo-Christian tradition says then love and being in love are a gift from God. It is something that we can celebrate and appreciate. Gratitude is an excellent way to help propel us to being in love and staying that way. So let's think some more about what happened when you first fell in love.

It was exciting getting to know every new detail. You enjoyed knowing what were his/her favorite brands, favorite music, and foods. Do you remember how exciting it was to just discover some new little quirk about them, or some similarities? Knowing that you both liked some of the same music, foods, people, movies etc was fun. And it felt like that both of you were quick to accommodate the other one. Do you remember how much you were willing to accommodate his/her moods, hopes, likes and dislikes? It was something that you were not only willing to do but excited to do, because you saw he/she was doing the same things for you. It was a magical time, was it not?

What were some of the things that attracted you to him/ her in the first place anyway? Was it because he /she were so cute, handsome or sexy, or were you only attracted after you got to know each other? Was it love at first sight, or did it happen over time? Was it a growing realization that you then suddenly acknowledged that you really liked being in their presence, or did it only happen when you thought you might lose them forever?

Whatever was the means it was a wonderful and magical time, when it seemed as if you had energy all the time and you were excited about tomorrow and the day after. It seemed as if the whole world was more accommodating and more fun to be alive. It was as if people seemed to be friendlier to you and acted as if you were someone they like. It probably was because your brain was giving off chemicals that altered your mood. You were high on being in love. You can be again and you can actually, chose it.

Your family was even easier to get along with. The people who in your family that seemed to get to you didn't bother you as much and they even seemed as if they were easier to get along with. It may have only occurred on occasions but it was as if even your family was treating you better. They probably were treating you better. You were in a better mood, were more tolerant of them and you obviously felt good. So the small slights any of them offered you overlooked and gave them back kindness and treated them as if they were just fine. They liked that because they probably didn't even know they had been insulting. When you were feeling good about yourself you even knew that or were very willing to believe they didn't know they were being insensitive because you had enough good feelings to go around for both you and them. In fact, your good mood probably helped your family to also feel good and so they probably were better to you than other times. It probably wasn't your imagination.

Now some of the good feelings were because of what you anticipated and some were because you were naturally doing and seeing things through a filter that can be consciously decided upon and recreated almost at will. It is something that God has built into us as created beings. We however don't always talk about it, even though it is there. I am convinced that this is something that God has wanted us to understand all along but somehow we haven't really grasp that this applies to both our relationship with God as well as with our partner. I think of this as part of a gift our faith brings us when we take the Bible seriously.

The hormones that our body produces when we are in love are wonderful. They help us have that amazing feeling where everything is ok. In fact, even more than that our hormones impact our immune system, and our whole way of being so we can be healthier, and happier. Being in that state perpetually can impact us powerfully in positive ways for all sorts of reasons.

The approach offered in this book will work as long as your relationship has enough left to rebuild, and given that your partner hasn't been having an affair, or become addicted to drugs, or has some other issue that would require psychotherapy. The good news is that even by using this approach you are more likely to become able to know whether improvement is even possible. Because how we see the world changes what we see as well as what we can see and how we see it. Some realizations change things and the way we see things. Certain emotions can expand or restrict our ability to see our own abilities let alone others abilities or restrictions.

Remember how you felt when you had some ah ha moment? Afterwards you almost couldn't go back to how you saw things before that moment. The new revelation made a difference while you might be able to go back to what and how you saw things before you would always have the awareness and that changes everything. That is part of what happens when we read the Bible or any sacred text and understand it in a new and powerful way, which adds to how we understand what is said to us.

You could take a few minutes right now to remember and recall things that you used to do, and how you related to your partner, as well as how you related to the world. Remember any of those moments as much as you would like to because you can have more of those times.

By remembering them you also are accessing some of the skills you were using back then to contribute to the overall success of the relationship. While we will go into this a whole lot more, even you're doing this simple exercise can help you to recover the skills you had when you were first in love. Because remembering some of those times actually puts you more in touch with the strengths that you have had all the time but may not have recognized them.

Now of course if you or your spouse is currently angry with the other one then there will be some work to do, to overcome that and there may be some other glitches that could get in the way but you already have the ability to fall in love so later we will draw on that skill.

For now we may need to get on the same page as we discuss what else you can do to improve the relationship and what simple things can get in couples' ways that are easily fixed.

After you have put this approach into practice you may discover that the tools that you discover you have can also be used to enhance your relationship with God or truth as well as with other people who are important to you. If you pay close attention to theology you may also discover that it mirrors some profound things that are said to us in the Bible about God's stance toward us. The improvement of the one just may assist and amplify our relationship with the other. That is the intent and my hope as this is written.

Also by putting this approach into practice will likely cause you to feel better about yourself in a lot of ways even beyond feeling better about the relationship. You are much more likely to like yourself and appreciate the many ways that you can take care of yourself and your emotions. In effect this approach is inviting you to take a spiritual journey that can lead you to greater fulfillment and happiness.

What I think is really wonderful is that using the love you already know how to do is a shortcut to almost all of the other approaches to improving relationships. By utilizing what you already know how to do it bypasses all the other problem areas, and allows you to fix things quickly easily and, gives you tools for the future. You did it once and you can do it again. It is actually easier than you might think, once you know how to do it.

Love is the only force capable of transforming an enemy into friend.
Dr. Martin Luther King, Jr.

1 John 4: 7 Beloved let us love one another: for love is of God and whoever loves is born of God, and knows God.

CHAPTER 2
HOW COME THIS BOOK CAN HELP

Throughout the Bible you are being given the message that you are loved. Throughout this book you are going to be invited to recognize how you can love and invite that feeling of being in love and inviting love from your partner. Obviously not everyone who wants or says they have a great relationship with God does, and nor does everyone who says they want a great relationship with their spouse does. It is similar to how some folk's experience being loved by God. Some folks seem to get that message and they thrive. Others will tell you they have it and they have bitterness to show you how well they got it. Still others haven't seemed to get any of the message and they don't thrive. Whether you have that special type of relationship with God or not, you can have a great one with your partner. However, doing so just may help you to have a better relationship with God.

Some folks who get the message really sense God's love everywhere. For them it is in the beauty of nature. It is in the sounds of silence, and in the chaos of the city. God's love can be heard by them in the voices of animals, people, and in the melodic harmonies of many different forms of music. For them God's love is in the sunshine, rain, storms, and even in the quiet of night. The really talented ones can see how God's love is in the entire Bible, and it for them is in many if not most of the interactions they have with God, and many of the interactions with other people. They look forward to talking with God and are excited about the answers they will get. They even listen for God's voice in everything that others tell them as well as what they encounter in their life in the way of coincidences. They are seeing how well they are loved almost everywhere. They are thankful and appreciative. They seem to radiate that love and people are mostly drawn to them. If you are one of those folks then you are going to be blessed especially by this book, because it will help you to do even more of what you are doing that is working.

In effect, to whatever degree that you get it, and know that God loves you then you have the ability to be in love with God. You may even recognize that you are in love with God and it is one of those things that you are very proud of and that you preserve that love relationship in serious ways. It may be that you have some favorite ways to address God that are private and between you and God. You may have a special time or place to pray. You may only pray on special occasions because you believe that God knows so much about you that there isn't as much reason for you to tell God stuff. Whatever your practices are with God, it is working, or else you wouldn't be recognizing that God loves you. Whatever your approaches are with God they too can probably improve. Almost none of us are constantly in a state of being as close to God as we would like. Most of us come close and then seem to drift away before we move to get close again. It is an ongoing returning and drift that we notice only after the fact.

One woman I know spends time in prayer every day. Carrie as I will call her is one of the most powerful prayer warriors there is or ever has been. Carrie is upbeat, and always willing to learn. She loves God so much that she is always willing to discover more truth about the Bible and about God. Carrie is willing to improve herself because she knows that she is alright the way she is. But because she is already ok, she can strive to become better all the time. She does. If you spent time with her you would catch her spirit of excitement for God. You would feel the sense of awe and love for being so loved and cared about. You would recognize that her enthusiasm is real. Her upbeat attitude is for real and so are her insights, facts, and how she loves to learn about the Lord. She is easy to care about because she is so willing to care about you, almost no matter what.

If you thought that Carrie has had an easy life you would be wrong in the sense of events that have been unpleasant. However, if you saw her life through her eyes it has been wonderful. That is because of how she views things. It may even be because of the things that she has overcome that she has such a wonderful attitude.

I know another woman whose idea of love of God is very different from Carrie's. This woman who I will call Elizabeth would see the joy the first woman has and it might inspire her but she probably wouldn't show it in some emotional display. The reason is that for Elizabeth actions are more powerful than words. She demonstrates her faith in things she does, and in ways that she treats others. She is so willing to be in love that she is in love with many of the people that the Lord created. Elizabeth is so clear about how much she knows that the Lord loves her, if she was to demonstrate it would be powerful to any who noticed how much she puts her faith into practice. It would be in her showing that same type of love or actions toward others, and in doing little things as well as bigger things for people because she believes that is important. She does it willingly and with much intention. It pleases her that she can do for others. She isn't co-dependent on what others say to her. She actually enjoys helping.

Actually, if you were to read or talk with folks who are very deeply in love with God you would notice they have wonderful times of prayer, and of communing with God, in thoughts, actions, and in reading the Bible, as well as attending worship services. What you would also discover is that many of them also have some doubts, or have periods that are not wonderful and others that they either doubt or they just don't have that same level of feeling that was so wonderful. It is because our emotional state of mind about God is influenced by the circumstances of our life. If everything is going well we tend to not think about God quite as much and then in a short time our relationship is not as rich.

It is a very mature person who realizes that their relationship with God is based upon their thoughts, actions and assumptions as well as how they interpret life, events, and the Bible. In other words it is about our actions and everything that goes into our doing what we do. We are responsible for how we interpret events in our lives. Even if God were to speak directly to us and give us directives personally, we are still responsible for how we would interpret the event. Our willingness to interpret events as from God is about our willingness to do so. Our willingness to recognize that we are responsible for how we interpret everything in our lives points to our maturity, and mental health.

Time can change how we continue to understand events in our lives. The events are not static just because they happened in the past, how we continue to interpret them has as big of an impact on us as the event itself.

Many people interpret even events that at the time that were interpreted as miraculous may not be later. Time can dampen a person's commitment to understand that dream, circumstance, coincidence, or miraculous event, as something from God. It is a decision a person has to make ultimately. When the event is long since passed and the emotions are gone, ultimately you have to decide how to interpret the events of your life. Was, or is God being present to you in the moment, or are you going to interpret it as your imagination? It is always that decision or some variation of it that determines how we understand events in our life and our relationship with God. The truth is that we always have to make that decision, and we have to live with the reality that is created by our decision. In fact, our decision creates the reality that we then live, because we decided it that way.

If that seems unfair, it may be. It is also as clearly the way that things are that I can tell. To think that there is some objective reality that we sense and know is to set ourselves up as an arbitrary judge, because it implies that we know and can know how reality actually is and it of course is how we see it. We all know people who see politics differently. Two people from opposite parties can both see the same thing and understand the events totally differently. Perhaps we are even sophisticated enough to realize that our take on how and what events mean says more about our projections than about reality.

I am reminded of studies where a panel of people all see the same car wreck, and then are told the wreck involved a young woman and an older man. The age and gender of the panel will determine ultimately how they will see the wreck. Some will see the same events as proving the older man was at fault, while others will claim the young woman was totally to blame.

Perception changes even what we can see or believe that we did see. Perception and reality are really that fickle.

Unfortunately in this culture we tend not to realize that our decisions about how to interpret something impact us in powerful ways. The person who decides to interpret as miraculous the event where God did something they first thought as miraculous tends to find amazing things in their life. However the reverse is also true. Folks who continue to interpret events first as miraculous and then re-decide that it couldn't be miraculous for some reason that disqualifies the event as miraculous or not tend to not have the best relationship with God as they could. The reason is that they are committed to doubt more than belief. They don't know how to cope with the doubt which assumes that if it can't be proven that it should be doubted. Taking that approach is one to protect us from feeling foolish, by avoiding believing anything that others may not also believe. However it costs a person any sense of the miraculous ultimately. While it seemed prudent to discount the miraculous part of the event, to protect them from being made fun of, they didn't see the price they would pay for not giving themselves the joy of discovering miraculous events.

Recognizing that our choices about what we are going to believe possible limits or opens up what we can see is about accepting how reality actually works. Our beliefs are that powerful as to alter our reality.

I know a number of people who are absolutely convinced that God is directly involved in their lives in amazing ways. They feel loved and cared about and somehow things always seem to work out for them in ways that are blessed. They do this in spite of the people who could and would find ways to explain away all of the wonderful events that convince them they are loved by God. Are they simply fooling themselves? Well if you call living in ways that are fulfilling, happy, and joyous as fooling themselves, perhaps. But the people who criticize them are seldom as happy, or confident. How do you answer the fact that their marriages are solid, their lives are content and they really enjoy themselves? I say they know things that all the rest of us could learn from.

What is it that they do that others don't do? They are willing to interpret coincidences and events in their lives as being from God, and they are determined to look for the blessing that God has for them, no matter what. If a door is closed they look for how God is going to bless them in another way. They may look for a window, another door, or some creative opening that simply just seems to appear. They seek those special coincidences when circumstances seem to tell them that they are cared about. It is what gives them their sense of being special. They love it, and probably wouldn't talk to just anyone about it because it is so special to them that they wouldn't risk telling someone who wasn't willing to believe.

One of the first times I met a woman like this, I was certain that she was deluded. I thought she was so naïve, that I had a difficult time taking her serious. Then I discovered that she had been volunteering on a terminal cancer ward every week. She wasn't seeing the world through rosy glasses because of her being naive it was me that was naïve. She was choosing to see the good that could be there and doing whatever she could to make the world a better place. She used courage to see the positive in spite of the fact that she saw what else was there. She was a wise woman.

Now I know a number of people who are willing to see and look for how to make the world a better place and who also work at looking for what is good about others as well as around them.

When we are willing to be responsible for what we chose to see then we are also able to discover how incredible that things can be, even when we are also acknowledging that there is pain and suffering in the world.

One of my favorite book titles is "Pain is inevitable, Suffering is optional". The Authors make a compelling case that pain in a part of life, but whether we suffer or not is a matter of how we understand the meaning of the pain, and how we think. The authors condense their book into the meaning of the title. They also said some profound things in the text.

Hypnosis research shows that the above is not only a good title but a simple truth and both point to a further truth. What we believe raises or lowers our immunity and ability to bounce back after trauma. How we view what our partner says, or what others say to us makes that big of a difference. It is amazing that changing how we understand a sentence from our partner can make that big of a difference. However, one small example can show this.

Bob: What are you wearing tonight?
Carol: What do you think I would embarrass you? (It is likely they will fight, raise their heart rate, and say things that neither of them would enjoy.)

Bob: What are you wearing tonight?
Carol: Are you going to match me? You know I love it when you do, and even when we contrast each other. (It will depend on how he responds but she has offered a possible way for them to go to a better place. At least right now their heart rate would not be elevated.)

Bob: What are you wearing tonight?
Carol: Oh honey, I love it that you want to know. You are so thoughtful and caring. (It is likely that with this response both parties will be secreting oxytocin and feeling more positive toward each other.)

Obviously, if either one interpreted the others words as a slight, or as controlling and responded that way it wouldn't go very well.

It is always that simple and yet that profound about how we interact. Our responses have that much ability to drive and direct where the relationship and this round of communication is going.

"There is always some madness in love. But there is also always some reason in madness." - Nietzsche

CHAPTER 3
SO THEN WHAT HAPPENED

There are debates about what happened, not just at your house, and in your head, but also with the experts. Some experts say that the positive things that I am going to tell you about are not only possible but a clear follow through of things we are discovering in the areas of trance and relationship. Others may say the levels of positive relationship that I am going to offer you are impossible, but then for some experts it may be because of their limiting frame of mind. Just last week I read an article about how being in love long beyond the honeymoon is a romantic notion but that adults know it isn't possible. I can tell you from personal experience it not only is possible but easily attained. Even last week a client called me and said ecstatically, "Guess what?" I am in love with my husband again." For our purpose what really happened that caused the problem is probably some combination of things, and isn't that important to me because it wouldn't help us get there any quicker if we knew, in some ultimate sense. How to make changes and get to where you want to with your relationship is important. We can explore what went wrong in a general sense so that it makes sense to do what we are going to do to restore and repair your relationship. That way we can all be on the same page and understand each other well.

Just the other day I read one expert that said, it wasn't possible to remain in love, and then a few pages later said, something quite different. The author said, "However, some lucky couples remain able to keep romantic love alive through the decades." The author said no one knows how to do it and then surmised it was genetic. It isn't. You are going to know how to do it in a little bit.

The poets and philosophers can debate what happens that causes two people to stop being in love. Who started, it or how it began or continued isn't as important as what you can do about it. Each of you unilaterally began the decline. You did so by your responses to each other, and you continued it by reacting on what you were afraid your partner said rather than what they may have really meant to say or what you would like for them to have said. You can unilaterally begin the ascent. This is not manipulation. This is not about manipulating your partner into being more of what you want but you becoming more of what you want. It is about using principles that can give you that feeling of being in love. This is about you getting back to what you already having proved works. You can improve the relationship at least on your side as long as your partner isn't secretly doing things he/she shouldn't. And you will be reversing at least your part of whatever brought the problem about in the first place, because you will be taking a stand and doing something about what you can, yourself and your attitudes. You can be proud of what you are doing.

It may have happened because we each individually began to blame the other for our own unhappiness. In fact, many people secretly believe that to be happy their partner must be a certain way. Oh, if we asked them outright they would deny it but they do. However it happened, whoever tricked us into believing that we had to have our partner be a certain way for us to be happy? It was a lie. We may have told it to ourselves because we didn't want to make the changes that we know and knew we needed to make to be really happy, so we wanted our partner to change. It may be that we get caught up in thinking that way because our culture tends to teach us such things indirectly in attitudes, movies, and songs. It may be that we got to the place of loving but not being in love because of the images of our parents, or other couples that we think are the standard for relationships, or the opposite of what we want. So the first place we may want to look would be at our self and whether we are angry or frustrated because of something we are not doing ourselves. Lots of people become angry with their partner because the partner doesn't make everything better. It is easy to see that they thought their partner would fix things and they didn't. I am not sure our culture doesn't set us up to believe that they would fix everything.

We are not taught to be responsible for our own feelings and our own happiness. If anything our culture teaches just the opposite. Where would we realize that being angry at our partner or blaming them simply wouldn't help any more than just blaming ourselves? When many people around us blame their spouses and partners for all sorts of things, we don't have a lot of examples where people deal with their issues and refuse to blame anyone. One reason we don't have a lot of those examples is that isn't going to attract our attention. It is something that happens and isn't bragged about or even made fun of. If you didn't even know to look for it you wouldn't have seen it even if it was in front of you. Besides if your parents didn't provide you with an example where were you going to receive the model? Positively looking for solutions doesn't usually involve blaming anyone. It is simply looking for solutions that will work. Of course very few of us would like to admit that the reason we have been angry with our partner has to do with what is inside of our own thinking.

There are lots of things that our culture teaches us that are not good for us but we are taught them anyway. It is commonly understood that our culture's attitude about junk food and or all sorts of things isn't good for us. We don't easily talk about those things. We don't always talk about the common beliefs that our culture offers as truths that are not so, but there are a number of them that get in our way to having satisfying relationships. Unfortunately, the cultural untruths are not easy to speak about it in generalities without stepping on toes. Take for instance how our culture and news programs imply what news is worthy. Usually it is often tragedy, scandal, or some natural disaster. There are lots of things that go right in the world that are not news worthy because they are not going to raise ratings for the news folks. It is a perspective that the news folks are presenting along with what they label as the events of the day. It may be subtle but that attitude impacts how we see the world. Do you intentionally look for the good things in your partner's make up behaviors? It is a choice to focus on those events or on others. That choice done in public actually impacts all of us in indirect ways because it is implying things to us without saying them out right. That happens a lot in movies, songs, and TV programs. Attitudes that are accepted without question have a way of impacting us without our conscious awareness. Many of the things that block our real happiness can be traced to beliefs that are accepted without question because it is so much a part of our culture. Probably most folks believe that the average millionaire makes a lot of money, and spends a lot of money, when that is mostly false. Most millionaires are very frugal and remain mostly frugal even after they have amassed a lot of money. Most of us who grow up in America have attitudes that make it much more difficult to become wealthy than do immigrants. It is because of beliefs that have seeped into our collective consciousness from our culture. Our culture invites a consumer mentality, not a saving one, or one that views money with a singular meaning. When multiple meanings of money are the basis of thinking then it is very difficult to manage, make or keep it very well.

It is very similar to how simply accepting things from our culture about love, relationships, and how we can act around each other is also not helpful. Fixing either the mindset about money or relationships is easy. It simply involves altering how we view it and respond. It is a mindset that when we adopt it we can be successful, in either arena. Ok, it is a little bit different mindset that helps with money than relationships, but both are very simple.

Another belief that blocks our relating well is almost universally accepted. That belief is that when you marry you can then talk about your in-laws just like their blood relative might. It seems so accepted that many people are shocked to realize that talking about their in laws to their spouse not only doesn't work it makes their relationship unpleasant. Consider that if I tell you how bad your mother treated me what can you really do about it? You can't fix the problem. You can sympathize with me or you can defend your mother. The only other options are that you can remain indifferent. You can't forget whatever I said easily and it is as if you now have a hot potato and no easy way to deal with it. It also didn't help me much to complain to you about your mother, because ultimately my relationship with her is my relationship with her. If you think about it very much you might conclude that talking about anyone in your partner's family isn't helpful to either of you and you might even decide that telling how angry you are with someone in your family to your partner doesn't help either. If as you read this you find yourself disliking what is being said it may be because you have swallowed more about how this is supposed to be ok from our culture than you might have thought. The unpleasant feelings may be your growing awareness that you can make changes that will positively impact your life in the future.

One study I am aware of looked at life satisfaction and television viewing; the more TV viewing the less life satisfaction that was reported. The reason was simple. What is the purpose of TV? Is it for entertainment, or is it to sell products? Would the shows be on TV if there wasn't a product to sell? What really hit me was that we are more likely to purchase a product if we are dissatisfied with our life. If you examine most programs offered on TV you will notice that you tend to feel less than the people displayed. It is a subtle thing but it happens. Most of us do not have a film crew following us around. We also don't have a staff of writers giving us material to use that is funny, witty, or informative. When we compare ourselves and our lives to those of the people on TV it is difficult to not come up feeling a little bit dissatisfied with what we are doing. It can even eclipse what we believe we can do when we compare our lives with other people. Comparing for evaluation of self ultimately leads to bad feelings. Comparing ourselves so that we are more motivated to do more almost always works well.

The truth is we each are responsible for what we chose to focus on and for our own happiness. As I understand it Jewish tradition says that is the purpose of life. Each person is to pursue their own happiness. Now the catch that the Rabbis know is that ultimate happiness can only be achieved by living within moral boundaries, and that means being in relationships with others, and with a moral code. Ultimately for the believer that also means being in a relationship with God.

Whether we want to admit it or not most of us go through being hot and cold in our relationship with God. Oh we would say that we fear God, or that we love God but we don't always feel really close to God. We have times that we are much more attuned and involved in actively doing the things that we know will make us and keep us in a good relationship with God, and yet at other times we are lax. We almost expect that sort of ups and downs in our relationship with God, but we don't' expect that type of wax and wane in our relationship with our partner. We get preoccupied, distracted and only realize it after the fact. When we realize we are not as close we can decide whether we want to get close again or not, but more often than not our perspective keeps us from it is knowing what to do to fix the problem. I have no idea how many very intelligent people who I know that do not know how to fix the problem of their relationship with God. They keep waiting for God to make the first move. It isn't surprising because it isn't easily known how to make the next step always. We are not taught how to because it is a little different for each person. Ever wonder how come most of the miracles in the Bible were only performed once? The situation is different each time and each of us is also different. It is about actions and intentions on our part, and our persistence that makes the difference.

Most of us know in our heart that we can improve our relationship with God on our part but we just are not sure what to do first, and we are scared of looking like a fool, or being some religious nut. Oh sure we might think we know exactly what we should do, but we still don't. One reason we don't do what we know we should is that we don't' know what to do after that. It is scary to not know the next step. With our partner we may well have tried the same things over and over only to feel as if there wasn't anything we could do. I believe that the thing that makes the biggest difference comes from what we want rather than what we are afraid of happening. Unfortunately, we mostly act on what is frightening us instead of what we want to happen. It is much more of the intent and desire of our heart and the honest actions that we take when we are being very honest with ourselves that makes the difference. It is also being humble enough to learn and not expect ourselves to know something that we haven't been taught. That is the image of the righteous person in Proverbs. He/she is willing to learn and discover how they can improve.

Why talk so much about improving our relationship with God in a book about staying in love forever? It is easy; it is because they are similar. Improving our relationship with God involves improving our response to boundaries that are put forth in the belief systems that we embrace. We would do that by recognizing them and analyzing them if we disagreed with what we believed was required of us. Sometimes what we believe is required and what is actually is significantly different. It means looking at what we disagree with and how come. Is it simply because we don't want to be hampered, or is it because our experience has shown that what we believe is required isn't in keeping with either the spirit of the Judeo-Christian tradition or with good relationships. If that is the case then perhaps we were misled by the cultural expression of faith, because a way of understanding the Judeo-Christian tradition is that the spirit of it is always leading to more blessings in life, by keeping us from making foolish mistakes.

In a similar way to improve our relationship with our partner will also involve our respecting rules that really work and not the ones that our culture has implied to us that don't.

If for no other reason than your own happiness and satisfaction you can improve what you experience from both God and your partner. Because let's face it, you aren't really proud of some of the things you have said or thought in anger at your partner. You really aren't proud of the negative things or hurtful things that you said, or thought about or even the things you contemplated doing are you? If you have some sense of embarrassment shame or remorse for what you have either said, done, or wanted to do then you are ready for this book.

Why am I mentioning both God and your partner in the same breath? Often how we treat the one will bleed over to how we treat the other. Few people can treat their partner well when they treat others badly. According to the Bible we are unlikely to treat our partner better than how we treat our God. How we treat God is pretty important about how we treat others. It is also important to realize that our relationships are bound by the ability to change and grow. They are also living and breathing and they will change. However, just blaming our partner or ourselves ultimately isn't of any more help than simply blaming God, for our predicament.

Probably one of the things that got you into not feeling in love with your partner was that you were being loyal to what our culture says is true. Our culture teaches a lot of lessons about relationships that are not helpful. Things like opposites attract, or jealousy is a sign of love, are widely held beliefs that are not backed up by science. Jealousy is more of a sign of not valuing ourselves and or comparing ourselves to others, than any sign of love. If anything jealousy is more of a sign of the lack of love, but our culture doesn't seem to see it that way. Another disbelief often accepted without question is that of opposites attracting. While some people seem to be attracted to someone who is the opposite of themselves generally people are attracted to people who look like themselves. However, if you simply accepted these things as so at some point you have been highly aware of what our culture implies to us.

Your ability to perceive what is implied by our culture is a strength that can become an asset for you even if all our culture teaches isn't true, or useful. For instance, one thing most of us glean from popular attitudes is that if you are right that must make me wrong. Few of us go around and tell others that both of us can be absolutely right even if we disagree. Now you probably agree with me that one of you being right doesn't make the other one wrong, but in practice especially when one of us is feeling blamed, ashamed or one down the disagreement becomes an indictment. How that idea that only one of us can be right ever got started is probably beyond being able to be traced, but it of course isn't even remotely close. However, while we are arguing, or one of us is feeling one down we can easily act as if only one of us can be right. When either one of us acts that way both of us can begin to even if we didn't consciously think about it. That is simply a feature of arguing. Of course we both can be right, and in fact both usually are, but that is for another time.

Probably one of the most pervasive beliefs that restrict and make our relationships dwindle and fissile is the belief has to do with reality. Most folks accept as given the reality they experience in their own skin. They assume that is the same for everyone else as it is for them. Most folks act as if whether they would say they believe there is an independent reality that exists that anyone can point to and proclaim what it is. That is so much the case that many folks see something and then declares what it means, even if they have no idea about what someone else is really feeling. It works like this. You are angry about some driver that is driving poorly and I can see the anger in your face, I reason that you must be angry with me, and when you speak to me it is still with that angry voice, so now I am certain. You are angry with me, and I speak to you with anger in my voice to protect myself from what you might say. It begins an escalation that seems to have little room for any disagreement.

Some folks refer to this as first and second order reality. First order reality of sky, earth, etc gets confused with second order reality that comes from what we declare the meaning of something to be. So that over time people come to feel something and assume it is reality when how they thought of and framed the meaning of what they saw is what created how they experienced reality.

The way it tends to work is that I am certain that I am right and no amount of your telling me that you weren't angry with me will change my mind, because I saw your face and I heard your voice. I am certain that I know what I know. I decide that you were angry with me! It doesn't matter that you were angry with the driver who passed by us minutes ago. I am positive you are angry with me and I start complaining to you or blaming you for being angry all the time with me. The more that you deny it the more I know you are also lying to me, because I am certain that you are angry. You see how far off the logic is? My deciding that your angry look and tone are about me is just my fear, and projection. It may not have anything to do with you. Because our culture doesn't even check this nor help us to know that our beliefs that way get in our way, it sets us up.

We are even encouraged to believe that what we remember is exactly the truth. Isn't that how we treat eye witness accounts? Courts know how unreliable memory is but still they persist. Memory is very malleable. In fact, emotions, desires, hopes, fears and even who we are and what we have been will influence what we will be able to see as well as what we remember.

It isn't something that is pretty. But it is pretty amazing that we actually believe something so far from what is verifiable. While we are not angry, hurt, sad, or afraid we can see this as nothing more than a misunderstanding. Add in my feeling hurt and my response and we are spiraling out of control. That out of control feeling or the arguments all came from what can be understood as a negative trance.

Why refer to the inability to relate to others as a negative trance? Because it makes things pretty simple to fix, and avoids any pointing of blame, and gives us ways of stopping the feeling that we are having at the time. Besides it also allows us to have experienced the emotions and not taken them personal. If the thing bothering me is a trance state it isn't me. It is a mental state that can be changed. There is plenty of blame for our culture, and what we are not taught regularly. Blaming each other doesn't help and won't fix anything. In fact, the more I blame you the more I will feel guilt. No amount of blaming you will fix my guilt. My blaming you actually, keeps it going. I know that isn't something that you learned before and it challenges your beliefs perhaps, but that is the way it works. At a later time I will explain how come, but for now...

Over time you either discovered ways to cope and argue or you didn't, but much of the time your arguments took on characteristic paths, and you would like for them to stop. Perhaps your arguments have only degenerated into fighting some of the time but you would like to have that in love feeling back.

You may even have given up on the idea that you could be "in Love" again. I saw an article just the other day that said staying in Love was impossible. I thought how sad that more people don't know about this approach. Perhaps you figured that you are doing as well as it can be. You can always point to the people who are arguing and fighting all the time. Besides most of us have heard about the stages of love and assume if we are beyond the "IN LOVE" stage that it is all over. While there is some truth to stages of love in that longer love that has matured is more satisfying that however won't take away from how satisfying the feeling of being "in Love" can be even with a mature love. I can testify to this and can point to couples who have done it.

However, right now we are talking about how the strain happened to your relationship in the first place. Let's admit that what all the therapists ultimately say about how come this happened from our backgrounds, or the way we structure our relationships or what we do in them is probably true. What this book is about isn't arguing with any of those theories. I am not disagreeing with any of the therapeutic approaches. This path seems to bypass many of the obstacles and gives you back the ability to do what came naturally. You have it already inside. The things the theorists say are helpful and have contributed to this book. Much of who I am and how I think has come from studying the various approaches. Another truth is that there is nothing new under the sun. Most approaches are variations of things that others have said.

I have no argument against any of the schools of thought. Almost every change that is offered by schools of thought is focused on one aspect or another of your experience. I find much to like about almost every approach I see. In fact, I love getting to learn new approaches. Some focus on thoughts, some on emotions, while some structure experiences so that you will relate more effectively on your own. Each is attempting to show a path to relating in a more effective way. All ultimately lead to improvements for folks. All of the schools of thought can help you achieve an improved relationship with your partner.

Because each one focuses on a different aspect of your experience each one has a tendency to be more helpful to some and less to others. Evidence based approaches not withstanding some approaches and some therapists can be more effective with certain types of folks.

I believe that what follows is a way of streamlining the process because it is utilizing the strengths and abilities you have already demonstrated. This approach will focus on utilizing the skills and strengths you have already demonstrated when you fell in love. If you aren't sure you ever did, following the simple guidelines can give you the experience of falling in love. From that point and by being able to maintain that point you can maximize your happiness and feel in love with your partner as long as you would like.

This approach is more about giving you quick tools to improve what will ultimately be your communication, your relationship and your feelings of satisfaction. It will even offer to you more personal satisfaction but not because anyone complied with you but that you took care of yourself using rules that really work. It is about what you can do rather than what you didn't do right. I find focusing on what we can do to improve where I like to spend my time. It improves my success rate. The folks who have used this method have usually been very happy that they did.

My life has no purpose, no direction, no aim, no meaning, and yet I'm Happy. I can't figure it out. What am I doing right?
Peanuts
Snoopy (Charles Schultz)

CHAPTER 4
WHEN YOU WERE "IN LOVE" YOU DID IT RIGHT

When you were in love you did it right without even knowing how or even what you were doing. The skill is still inside of you. What you did right before you can use again. Think about how much better you can be when you are doing those things more intentionally and more consistently so that you get what you want. If you were naturally good at it before without even knowing what or how you were doing what you were doing then knowing how to generate that emotional state can make a powerful difference.

In spite of what some objections to being in love that our culture says it was a wonderful time. You know some of the foolish things our culture says about being in love. Popular wisdom claims that when we are in love we are blind to each other's faults, and that we see everything through rose colored glasses. Our culture is in effect criticizing a couple's ability to overlook each other's faults and to focus on the good qualities. It is a disdain for what being in love can do for a couple that is being criticized. It is also a sour grapes sort of attitude from people not in love. If you think about it being respectful of each other is really about being able to overlook each other's flaws. In fact, a part of mental health is being able to not get hooked and angry about things that would bother us.

I looked up the origin of the love is blind idea and Shakespeare was being very bright as always with his observations. It is fascinating how our culture has changed the meaning of what Shakespeare said, and used it to mean what the culture says. Over time folks add or take away from what he actually said, in a lot of ways. I simply found this one particularly relevant. I found this quote attributed to him.

Author: William Shakespeare
But love is blind, and lovers cannot see
The pretty follies that themselves commit.

If you are interested it is from The Merchant of Venice. ACT II Scene 6.

That is a very astute observation that lovers are blind to their own follies, and a very different one from love is blind. Actually, the idea that lovers are blind to their own follies is a good thing from our perspective, because pointing out your partners mistakes seldom causes them to change in any positive way. Besides being blind to my mistakes and choosing to be blind to my partner's mistakes makes life easier. In fact, I would argue that critically telling each other our faults tends to make us dig in our heels and become more adamant that we are right. When criticized it can feel as if our past and everything we hold dear is being questioned. When someone makes the pronouncement that we are wrong and they don't even know our past and how come we came up with what is being criticized it can feel as if it is about our whole person.

Criticism usually only heightens their wall to you and anything you might say, or they counter with something about you that you don't like and an argument ensues. There is a little bit of balm that comes from not having to see, or be so intensely aware of our own mistakes. I think it is there because being so aware of our own mistakes can cause us to be more aware of our partner's mistakes as well. Usually people who are intensely aware of their own mistakes can site chapter and verse about our mistakes if angered.

Being willing to overlook mistakes our partner makes is an incredible skill that leads to deeper relationships. As you continue to read you may discover that you have more ability to do that than you may realize. It doesn't mean that we don't want to teach and guide our partner to become more responsive to us, or to be more responsive to our signs of affection. It means that we are being strategic about it. In fact, contrary to popular wisdom that not noticing your partner's mistakes means that you have to accept them forever, it often leads to them wanting to change for the positive. They did when you were in love. It even can and does lead to our partner making and wanting to make changes to make us happier. It is because of your accepting of me that makes me want to be a better person. It usually isn't because I was soundly criticized.

Sam Keen said, "You come to love not by finding the perfect person, but by seeing an imperfect person perfectly." (Sam taught at Louisville Presbyterian Theological Seminary before his career at Psychology Today.) I think he is right. Sam has a reputation for saying two things at a time. I think he is saying that seeing an imperfect person as perfect makes us be in love. I think he is also saying that seeing an imperfect person completely is to love them. Both ideas are true and together they imply that love is an intentional act of love committed to overlooking the flaws and sometimes by knowing the partner so completely that we love with a willingness to overlook any flaw. One of the most powerful ideas in the Bible is that God loves us, and that love comes through in the laws, in everything in the scriptures if you are looking for it. It however is there for us not because we are perfect but because we are loved. If however a person wanted to not see God as loving or didn't have the capacity for accepting a God then that person would not find it. We can only discover what we have experienced or are looking for. If you are looking for it then it can be found in the first book onward. We become acceptable in the sight of God because God already loves us and forgives us. We are forgiven not because we are able to be completely good, or even that we deserve to be forgiven. We are loved. On a practical level I don't even see flaws in my wife. If she even has them I don't' see them. I am however truly grateful that she overlooks mine.

Here is another quote that says a lot with a little.
Author: William Shakespeare
Love sought is good, but given unsought is better.

Twelfth Night. ACT III Scene 1.

When we desire to be loved we desire a good thing. When we give love without regard to being loved back that is even a better thing. It doesn't matter whether it is to our partner, or to the next person we meet on the street. Our willingness to love another person impacts us in a very positive way. An argument could be easily made that loving someone else is better for the person loving than being loved. That isn't a popular idea. In fact, no matter how true it is many people won't believe it. Most folks experience and believe that being loved is more important to them than loving. They just don't get it. Some studies that I am aware of about our having a pet indicate that having a pet reduces the amount of stress we experience. It also has many other positive results. The center for disease control says that Pets can decrease your:

Blood pressure
Cholesterol levels
Triglyceride levels
Feelings of loneliness

The way that happens is by your loving the pet, not the pet loving you.

It translates into our human relationships as well. If we are focused on the love we can give to others we feel better, healthier and more connected. Besides if we are focused on what we can give we are going to be blessed doubly, because focusing on being loved generally leads to disappointment, loneliness and health problems. The reason is easy to point to because focusing on our being loved means we have no power over making that happen, and we probably have different criteria than our partner for what that would look like. So our partner may be showing us the most amazing love in their way but we still could be disappointed because it isn't coming in the form that we anticipated. You might be surprised at how often that happens. The opposite is also true. You might be surprised at how often your acts of love bless and protect you.

I have seen many couples who were missing the love the other was offering and did offer. It was a major part of how come they were not as close as they could be. One or both kept looking for love in a certain way and it wasn't coming in that arena but was offered in another. They didn't see it. Because often when a person doesn't see it in the usual way they assume it isn't coming, or has been withheld. That of course isn't helpful. In fact, assuming that blames the other person for not doing or giving what we want and convicts them of an offense of withholding. It convicts them of a crime that they not only didn't commit but that they didn't even know they were being charged, let alone being convicted without any trial, or even being asked.

Now if instead of assuming that they didn't withhold love, I can assume that my partner is offering love but I am just not seeing it, then the world is an entirely different place. Consider that if they are offering and I don't see it but I am assuming it is there then I can look in other ways and in other places for what I believe is there for me. It is common that a person offers messages of love to their partner that are not seen. If I assume it is there then I can take care of myself and them by acting on my positive assumption. If I assume it is there and stop looking for it in the usual places and perhaps expect to see it in unusual places then I can still find it. Actually, my looking with the expectation of finding it will in fact, cause me to be abler to find it. Expectation actually, induces a mild trance, and that can even alter how our brains work, and can understand things.

If I decide to be certain it is there then I can offer love also in ingenious ways and I will begin to feel much better. I may actually begin to feel quite wonderful. Especially, because my assuming it is there will make it either so that I can see it in what you do, or that you will respond to the positive I offer in such a way that I can assume you appreciate me that much and there is my proof. That is true even if I didn't see your love of me in the usual places that I was looking. It is also true that when either of you are feeling love toward the other one it is also very possible that it can then be felt by the other one. You can expect that when you were in love you did it that way. Yep!

When you were in love you did it right. You sought to show love and interpreted everything that your partner did as meaning they loved you. It was just a natural response you had to being in love and wanting to do for your partner. You simply responded to what he/she said as if you knew they loved you and your response implied you loved them back as well. It was automatic, and your desire to show love as often and as in as many ways was a goal you focused on and you beamed because you felt so loved.

We can laugh at examples of someone being that much in love. You know the way it goes.

He: I am so angry that I could see stars!
She: Wow! He really loves me. He has such strong feelings.

Or
She: (Red in the face) What are you wearing?
He: Wow! She really loves me! She cares about what I am wearing.

Or still another example of something more everyday.

He: Where are the car keys?
She: Wow! He really loves me so much he thinks that I even know where his car keys are.

We can laugh at the examples and that is the point. When a person is in love they see things different than a person who isn't in love. We can easily see in the first two examples how that a person would easily be almost or really overdoing it to interpret the events as love. Yet, in the third example the interpretation is more easily understood. However, all three are about interpretation. Our first interpretation of the meaning of anger, or interest in what we are wearing can be just as easily seen as a projection. When you have gotten angry at your partner was it because you loved them or because you didn't love them? That is right. It was probably because you loved them and were exasperated that they thought so differently than you think. We clearly project thoughts and feelings onto our pets. Well most of us who have pets do anyway. We ascribe feelings, thoughts and attitudes to them that we want them to have if they were to love us unconditionally. While it is true that many dogs are really bright and have a large vocabulary we really don't know if they feel the ways that we project them to feel. We just do it anyway and feel better about ourselves and them as a result.

Isn't it smart to at least treat our partner as well as we would our pet? When we get benefits from our pet it is because of what we offer the pet. It is still real. We still get the actual benefits and it makes us feel good. There are silly rules our culture teaches that negate our treating people at least as well as pets. In fact, a good friend of mine just sent me an article about how that we can learn from our pets how to treat our partners. The article advocated what I am here. It was also written for people who like and appreciate pets.

Ok, if you can stand it there would be a terrible pun about how come that we call our lover pet names. Because we treat them as if they love us because we love them and that is how we treat our pets.

If it works so well for our pets how come more of us don't do this with our partners? I think it is because we have cultural rules that practically sabotage relationship and other rules that are not so helpful for sustaining relationships. I tend to think of the rules as rules that make relationships difficult. Rules like the following.

Some Rules that make relationships very difficult if not impossible.

1) We must never be made to be the fool in a relationship.
2) We must never allow them to get the upper hand.
3) We must never be nicer to them than what they do back with us.
4) We must always try to keep the upper hand by not letting our partner know we love them more than that they love us.

The truth is that rules like the above and all of the other ones like those make it very difficult for us to sustain a relationship. If you ever wondered about some of the rules ask your same sex friends about relationships and the rules. Most folks have some rules that are less than helpful and yet are offered as sage advice for being in a good relationship. Some of the worst advice a man or woman can receive comes from their same sex friends, who mean well but are offering rules they live by themselves. That doesn't mean that everything your friends say is wrong, but when you are the most needy it is likely. If you ask your friends when you are not in need you can perhaps see the illogic of what they say. Often the rules are the things that make communication between partners difficult because of assumptions and expectations that are not openly discussed.

"That which is done out of love always takes place beyond good and evil."
- Friedrich Nietzsche

CHAPTER 5
TIPS FROM YOUR OWN EXPERIENCE OF LOVE

A useful way of thinking about what you did right would be something that helped give you the ability to recreate it without having to fall "in love" again. Falling implies that you didn't have control over it, and wouldn't know how to make it happen again, except through some big risk. It would be especially helpful if this useful way of thinking about your being in love gave you insights about what had kept you from being in that state of "in love" as well. I hope to do just that.

One way of thinking about what you were doing right was that you spontaneously developed a positive trance. One reason that this helps is that there are rules surrounding trances that can then be used to assist you achieving a positive trance of being in love, and keeping it going by clear rules that help. It also can mean that when you were not " in love" you were also in a trance and that too can be changed and isn't about you but the state of mind you were in. When you fell in love it probably felt like it was accidental or mysterious.. When you do it this time it will be because you are choosing for it to be something you experience. Trance states are something that we all go into and out of all the time. It isn't hypnosis but a trance that develops spontaneously. Hypnosis by most people's definition involves a second person leading the first by words and influence. It is a relational interaction. Trance and Hypnosis are not the same.

A practical way most all of use trances is in shortcuts for doing things repeatedly. It is a way of simply using your skills more efficiently. You are then able to think about something else and still do the repetitive task easily and quickly. Most people have shortcuts for doing something they have done repeatedly. Those are usually things you are able to do easily when you are in a trance. The repetition helps but it is a mindset. A really good tennis player plays in part by being in a trance where they allow everything else to move to the background and they are focused only on what they need to for being highly effective. We do it so that we can make shortcuts, and so that we can be more effective. Trances are something that we all go into and out of all the time. We however don't usually talk about them in those terms. It happens in part by what we immerse our thoughts and feelings in. Trance is defined by what we pay attention to and what we ignore. What we pay attention to is in the foreground of our attention and what we tend to ignore is in the background.

If for instance you watched a scary movie late at night by yourself and heard a strange sound outside you would think something quite different from what you would if you were with your friends, or watching something that was a love story. The emotions would cause you to think different thoughts. The line of thoughts that would follow from fear would be very different from feeling all loved and cared about. The fearful thoughts would lead you to very different conclusions than ones that happened when you were dwelling on thoughts of love, happiness, being grateful and looking forward to tomorrow. What you were paying attention to because of your feelings would alter what you saw, felt, heard and believed.

When we are staring off in space and distracted from things going on around us we are in a trance. We are focused on something so intensely that what is going on around us is of lesser importance to us than the thoughts that we are focused on. When we are feeling that time is slipping between our fingers we are in a trance, because time moves at the same rate, yet when we are in a trance state and focusing on the time moving fast or slow it is altering our perception of time. Feeling like it is going faster or slower is from our perception and that comes from our feelings and what we expect and are afraid of happening. When you habitually put your car keys in the same place and do so without even thinking you are probably in a trance. When you do many of the things you normally do that make your life easier because of your doing them naturally and habitually, you are in a trance. When people are distracted and afraid they are in a trance. When you are really doing well and fully aware of everything around you and perhaps even very effective, you are in a trance. You could easily see great artists like Beethoven, Mozart, as being in a trance while they wrote many of the pieces they wrote. You could think of great athletes, or performers as being in a powerful trance state that allows them to focus on what they are doing in ways that may seem extraordinary. People of any persuasion who are operating at a very high ability and mental state are probably in a trance where they are fully aware and fully functioning at their capacity. It is a very wonderful thing. Some folks speak about it as mindfulness, others as flow, and still others as many other things. For our purposes it is easy to think of those times as trance states.

What you were doing right was dwelling on what was good, right, beautiful, peaceful, excellent, and gracious about yourself, the world and your partner, well at least in part. You were dwelling on what was going on right. You anticipated good things and attributed good meaning to what he/she said. When you did that it made your responses elicit good responses back. It was a way of thinking that happened spontaneously when you were in a good mood, expecting good, and interpreting things that were said to you in a positive way.

One of reasons that thinking about this in terms of trance is so useful, is that it gives us easy ways of changing our trance and also of eliciting that positive place of being in love. It then becomes something that we are doing by drawing on what we already do well, and have done well. Trance happens from focusing on either foreground or background. What we are focusing on in the foreground and what we are only seeing in the background leads to what we actually see, and can see. If two people are looking at the same things but one is seeing one thing in the foreground while everything else is in the background they will see two very different things. It is in part what makes so much of a difference between what two people can see, because of habits of looking at specific things. When you have been short on time and needing to find something it may have been right in front of you but you still may not have been able to see it until you looked with different emotional and attitude toward what you were seeing. From a different perspective it may be easy to see. Knowing that trance is based upon what we intentionally focus on and what we also intentionally chose to overlook we then begin to realize we do have the power to alter trances that we experience. The more you realize this the more power you will have over the things in your life that bring happiness and what doesn't.

Most of us have tried to not feel a certain feeling. It didn't work very well did it? If however you were to acknowledge what you already feel and then add on to that feeling what else you are aware of that leads you to where you want to be then you will begin to feel what you want to feel. If you question this then notice how you shift from one feeling to another especially when the shift went from what you didn't want to what you do want. It is actually a principle that works quite well.

You could try it out right now if you would like. You will be able to see it best if you start with some intense feeling or awareness that you are feeling or experiencing. While you are aware of that sensation, you can also become aware of what you want as well as what is going on around you and the steps to getting where you want to be. While you allow yourself those experiences and sense of awareness you could also add on a sense of your own competency, ability and personal power, in addition to thinking about all of the above you could also allow yourself to become aware of how connected you are to your family, and the neighborhood, as well as friends. If you really allowed yourself to go to all of those places and add onto your awareness that you began with then you have altered what you began with in a profound way, by associating that sensation with all the other awareness that you were having.

If we talked about this in terms of our relationships then we could notice something quite powerful. If you decided to feel a certain thing and found yourself feeling it and your partner wasn't accustomed to you feeling that then you would be offered a powerful decision because where they are and their emotions wouldn't necessarily be supportive, so you get to decide how to respond to their being at a different place than you are. If we put that into a practical everyday occurrence it might take on practical meaning. For instance when we would be going along seeing things well and at some point our partner says something that sounds to our ears like they are being hurtful or unkind. Now when we are in a good mood we can say to ourselves, "Wow wonder what is going on with him/her? That isn't like them. "If however we were hurting already or doubting our ability at the same time they said something then we might have responded with something not so kind. Our response could then take what was a miscommunication into an argument. If instead we responded well to what was said as if they were saying something very positive then we would more likely get a positive response. When it was going well it was because we still chose to see the insult they said, or sharp comment as about them instead of about us. That kept us safe and it also allowed us to respond with a good response instead of one that would take both of us to a bad place.

What we were doing right was that when we were first in love we were so dwelling on how happy we were to be in love that we were able to interpret almost everything that our partner did that was good. When they did something that wasn't so good we continued to see the good in it and it helped keep them in a good mood, and so they responded more and more to our positive things as well.

What we are not taught in our culture is that our response to a comment is much more about us than the original comment was to us. Let me explain. Communication is said to be 93% context, innuendo, body language, facial expression, tone of voice and etc. Only 7% of communication is words. That means 93% of what we hear is really only in our heads a projection of what we are saying, thinking and feeling at the time. So any comment that someone else makes to us is far less about what is going on with them than it is about us because how we hear it is almost totally about us. Obviously I am not disagreeing that we often can and do read each other quite accurately. Your intuitive ability to read others may be very effective. There is evidence that neuroscience concurs with your being able to recognize things very well that are going on with others. What I tell people is that with strangers you may be very accurate and even with your partner on occasion. What happens is that your emotions whether fear, hurt, hope, joy, or even grief, sadness, or boredom do on occasion impact what you would see. When it does it is likely to lead to both of you having hurt feelings. Because of this the only way to really stay safe is to check what you see out with the person but even before doing that to recognize that whatever we want to see it as, can impact the situation powerfully.

If our partner is being intentionally hurtful and it is clear then we can also use the approach outlined here to respond. Yes this approach even works with intentional insults, and rude comments that were intended to be hurtful. When we decide to interpret them differently we can protect ourselves from those hurtful things as well. When I worked at the prison this was a very valuable tool to use on occasion.

One day in particular comes to mind where I was able to protect myself from hurtful things that were being said. An inmate who was in the Cell block for misbehavior became angry toward me when I went to visit her and others in the cell block. She started cursing and yelling at me every insult that she could think of and then repeated some of them again. There was no point to write her up for her behavior as she was already in the Cell block. She was miserable because of her own actions and so as I walked away from her and even away from the building I could hear her still cursing me because she was yelling by this time. Everyone else could hear it as well. The looks of people who were amazed that I wasn't letting her words and insults bother me was very flattering. I didn't take either the insults or the flattery personal. Neither were about me. Both the flattery and the insults were about the people saying them to me far more than about me.

Now I know that approach is a radical idea. It goes against everything we have lived with about communication most of our lives. We have told ourselves that something meant what we knew it meant. We didn't even question whether it meant what we decided it meant because we never had any reason to doubt ourselves or our ability to read people. It was clear to us in the context it meant what we thought it meant. That may have been a misunderstanding when it comes to our partners. Experts in communication are very clear that only 7% of communication is words. If you really think about it that makes our communication amazing that we can do it at all or with as few miscommunications as we have already. However, it also offers us a very real way of utilizing that for our benefit. If you begin to get used to this concept and allow it to teach you, then you will become very happy about yourself and what you can achieve. It offers lots of meanings about communication that can alter how we see the world.

I remember at the prison we had an inmate who said she was pretending to be an inmate but that she was really in a witness protection program. My first thought was, "And I didn't even see that she was paranoid." Everything she said to me sounded like an excuse and made her words sound more unbelievable. It made me question everything she said. It was so intense that I was even thinking of a treatment plan for her, to deal with her problem of paranoid thinking. While she was talking to me and explaining the elaborate means and reasons that she was in the witness protection program I was so suspicious that she must have felt my disbelief. At the height of that moment I got a phone call. It was the warden. She told me the inmate I was talking to was going to come to talk with me and that what the inmate said was true. She was in fact in a protection program and she was being protected. The timing of the remark shocked me and caused my head to spin. My world had just been turned upside down. This sort of thing just didn't happen. It never did to me again in that way, but it did in lots of other ways. I hope this event and others including the ones you have had points to how powerful it is that when we are seeing something and are accustomed to seeing it that way it is very difficult to change. Yet, it also points to how different the world looks with only a few facts. Knowing that what the inmate told me was true, I understood her totally differently.

You may know about the old joke about being wrongly locked up in an insane asylum and trying to tell an attendant that you don't belong there. Everything you would say would be interpreted as your being in denial. There is nothing you could say to an attendant that would convince him to let you free. His job would depend on seeing you as he sees you. Nothing you could say would sway him because no matter whether he believed you or not he would have a good reason to not believe you, because his job is on the line to not believe you.

Even though our response is about us, we have tended to believe it is about what we see or hear. It isn't. It is about our projection of what we heard, saw, felt, believed, and were prepared to see. We tend to rely on standard ways of understanding things and as a result are usually correct in obtaining the same types of beliefs that support the way we see the world. A good way of taking care of ourselves would be to recognize this fact of communication. Instead our culture likes to act as if whatever we think is what someone said is true and that we somehow have the actual meaning of what they said, and nothing they say can change that.

It brings us to two rules that I believe are useful for our maintaining and creating good relationships. Lots of philosophers, theologians have mentioned these rules but because they have been associated with rigid expectations, or obscure thinking or just not fitting the popular myths, they haven't caught on. First, that what we hear is more about our ears than about what the person said to us and that by taking responsibility for what we hear we can really choose in a major way where our relationship is going. I think it is partially because we are willing to take responsibility for our own projections instead of simply believing them and acting as if our projections didn't come from ourselves that gives us the power to change things.

When you were in love you were doing that naturally. When you were in love you were spontaneously seeing, thinking, feeling, and anticipating good things. When you do that again you get the same result. It happens because your response shapes what the other person then responds to and if your response to them implies you like and believe in them and then the communication partnership you are creating is going to be a good one. It happens naturally.

The second rule also isn't original but my take on it is and it has been useful to many who have adopted it. If you are right it doesn't mean that I have to be wrong. In fact, a better starting place for all of us is where we both recognize that we are and can be both right and search for how we are both right to begin with. By doing so we short circuit much of the unhappiness of arguments because when we think that the other person being right means that we are wrong we get defensive and become angry, and usually attack. Now, in a rational mind all of us can agree with this idea. It is when we are feeling attacked and our thoughts, opinions; feelings and history are screaming that we are being told we are wrong that we have a difficulty seeing the truth of this. That is precisely where the idea of trance comes in because it is a negative trance when we see only two options. Either you are right and I am wrong or you are wrong and I am right when we both are feeling scared, hurt, or defensive is a negative trance. A negative trance rationally doesn't see more than two options. The standard ones are bad and worse. One option is not so good and the other one is worse. When we notice that we can step back and discover how to become in a positive place where we can see more options.

Notice how much easier it is to think or talk about it when the two of you are not angry, defensive or hurt. Usually later when in a clear head we are more than a little embarrassed what we said, thought, and even didn't say. We still are a little hurt about what the other one said as well, and so it takes us a while to realize how much we really hurt each other because in our angry mood we justified our thoughts. Now, if you think about this in a rational way, when we were justifying things that later we know are not fair, or were put in a way that wasn't fair or hurtful we can also recognize that the mood of anger was a trance state that corrupted even what we thought so that it was distorted to a maximum pitch.

One man I came into contact with is a perfect illustration of this in the positive extreme. He was overworked and had been putting in 70-80 hours a week to help change over a system at his work place. He was going to have to attend a workshop in another city and he wanted to go early so he could have a day or two off. His boss told him" no" several weeks before the event. So he dutifully kept working and then went to the workshop. When he got to the city and checked into the hotel, he noticed the Hotel clerk seemed a bit odd to him. He shrugged it off and went to his room. In his room he then checked the brochure for the workshop, and discovered that he had in fact gotten to the city the day before he was supposed to arrive. He had been so certain that he was to be on the plane and to check in at the Hotel that both people hadn't even bothered to check. He was amazed that being so certain had gotten him to the city he wanted to go to and people hadn't checked his plane ticket or anything. He was truly inspired to live with more certainty so he might have things go his way more. The conference ended early and so he decided to try flying on a plane earlier than his reservations. He marched up to the desk and handed his ticket and was promptly told he would have to wait. His confidence and certainty was different. What had worked the first time wasn't even going to get close the second time. The man learned an important lesson and was the smarter because of it. He realized that when we are completely convinced we might convince someone else but when we are only trying to be convincing we usually convince no one. He also didn't lose his job because of his going early in the first place. All was understood and mostly treated with laughter, because of how honest that he was.

Another situation almost in the exact opposite result occurred because of assuming only in a negative style. This man and his wife had problems living within a budget. He wanted to blame her, and didn't pay attention to how much she spent or didn't spend. She took care of the finances and the books for his business which was lucrative but wasn't making the money he thought it should have. He got suspicious because the debts were not going down at the rate he believed they should. In fact, he thought they should be on easy street because he worked so hard and was making so much money. However, since he was in denial about his own spending habits he didn't count the stuff he was adding to the credit cards. Besides since she was in charge of the finances any time he asked questions his suspicion added to her defensiveness and that fueled his certainty. The more he asked questions and the more defensive she became the more certain he was that she was guilty. It wouldn't occur to him that his asking questions with a lot of emotion and accusing in his voice would almost guarantee defensiveness.

His suspicion then became even larger and began to even grow into other areas. He began to disbelieve in her love of him and even began to see it as an attack on him. He was able to think all of this without many clues, signs, or facts. His fear and perspective distorted everything that she said. When she was reacting to his pulling back he became more convinced she was using him. Everything she said became more ammunition in his eyes. It didn't matter if she defended herself, or if she pointed out what he spent, or how hurt she was for his accusations he became more and more convinced that she was using him. Worse still was that he began to see what he did for her as his being taken advantage of by her, and then everything that occurred was proof that it was happening. So when he saw things she bought for her kids, he was furious. He ignored the things he bought for his children. They both had been married previously.

Now, since I saw and had contact with both of them during some of this time I knew that there was a serious miscommunication going on. It didn't matter. I didn't have the language to help. I am not sure that I could have because I am also not sure it wasn't related to things not associated with each other. I didn't know how to help them at that time with this approach.

They both were in a negative trance and couldn't get out of it. I never knew whether he simply wanted out of the marriage and allowed this to happen or if he really had been so in denial that this spiraling of events happened anyway. He didn't want to take responsibility except in the abstract way for not looking at his books while she was handing the finances. Not doing so on a regular basis of course leads to unpleasant realizations.

No matter what she said, he couldn't hear her situation. It didn't matter how hurt she was at his accusations. It didn't matter how loyal she was at loving him or doing for him. She felt attacked. He felt betrayed. Whatever the other said was interpreted in such a negative light it led to the same conclusion. They both lost each other, as well as much else. It was one of those tragedies that I just couldn't help. I also hadn't thought of this approach and ways to help using the things that I am telling you now. Perhaps some other therapist could have helped them. Perhaps, I could have with this approach we won't know that. I never got much of a chance to do so because they both wanted to see me individually, and not with the other one around. Some of it was their work schedule, some of it was their distrust of each other. By the time I figured it out that it wasn't a case of dishonesty or betrayal, it was way too late.

It was too late not because both of them had said some very hurtful things to each other. That seldom helps but it was worse than that. Just saying things to each other that hurt wouldn't end the marriage. They had both said terrible things to their families and friends about each other. Again that would make patching things up more difficult but that didn't make the break final. Many folks make the mistake of saying things to their friends and family that can't be taken back and make any future relationship between the friends, family and the partner more strained than it was in the beginning. It was too late because he had started telling himself that he would be better off without her and that there were other women who would be happy to have him. He had his eye on a couple of women and was anticipating how wonderful his life would be with the new women.

Even that wouldn't have been the straw that did it because that too would be something that could be overcome. He simply didn't want to. That was the reason it was over. He simply didn't want to. She did even after all the hurtful things he said. Unfortunately, he interpreted her willingness to work on the relationship as proof that she just wanted to make a bigger fool of him. It helped him to be more able to leave her in the least destructive manner possible which is what I suspect he wanted. Actually, I hope that with the above discussion of sanity and proving our sanity to someone who disbelieves us, that it wouldn't have mattered what she said. He had made his mind up and was going to interpret whatever she said, and did as proof that he should leave.

The irony is that had he interpreted everything in a different way they would still be married, and probably very happy.

I know couples who have gone the exact opposite way and they are still together. They have new ways of understanding each other and they have new ways of dealing with arguments and they have confidence that they can overcome almost anything. That is of course true. Today, a former client called and left a message. She was ecstatic, and said, "I am in love with my husband" Before using some of these techniques she was not only not in love with him she wasn't even liking him very much.

Whether we are negatively projecting or positively projecting what our partner says and does it is still a trance, and that means it can be easily changed. It also means that whatever we see can add to the proof that what we see is right. One old saying that seems so true to me is that "Whether you believe you can or you can't you are right."

If I know what love is, it is because of you." - Hermann Hesse

CHAPTER 6
MARITAL HAPPINESS RESEARCH

A study I found originally sought to discover whether high or low expectations for marriage would help more. It is a classic argument that has been debated by the very educated and the uneducated alike. It has been debated by the famous and the not so famous. Many people want to see their favorite side win. The debate is over expectations and marital happiness. Does high expectations or low ones lead to more happiness in marriage? People have been debating this argument for a long time. The high expectations folks say that having high expectations leads naturally to having better hope, more room to grow and a positive experience because the positive attitude leads to more positive experiences. They want to parlay their positive hope and experiences into a hopeful and positive experience for themselves and their relationship. It has to do with ways they protect themselves. They believe it will help their relationship. If you are married to one of these folks they probably are frustrated that you don't share their belief that this attitude will fix things or at the very least help.

The low expectations folks say that not getting your hopes up leads to not being disappointed and therefore more quality relationships. Their goal is to not become disappointed and to live in what they consider to be more of a reality. They are guarding against disappointment. If you are married to one of these folks they are protecting themselves and hoping to avoid worse problems. They are taking the relationship very seriously. They are actually, doing what they know to protect themselves and you. They want to avoid the unpleasantness of arguing, and even want to avoid conflict. Conflict in their opinion seldom leads to a good place and so they may avoid it at all cost.

If you ask lots of folks they will come down on both sides of this classic argument. How we see it probably says more about our style of protecting ourselves than anything else. You can learn about your style and yourself especially by embracing the fact that whatever your answer was it was about how you tend to protect yourself. If you have high expectations you may enjoy the thrill of looking forward to better things and improvement. You may have an easy time protecting yourself from criticism because you live with encouragement inside of your own head. I really don't know but you can know and can appreciate your style.

The same is true of the folks who believe low expectations help better. They too protect themselves with this mindset. If you chose this then you probably are well aware of how cruel disappointments can be, and have figured a way to protect yourself from the pain of having your hopes up too high.

The way I remember the research was that it gave only a slight edge to the folks who had high expectations. It was so close the only edge wasn't really an edge unless you count the fact that it simply left open some possibilities the low expectations folks didn't think about. It wasn't significant. Whichever way you chose is and still can be right for you. Using this approach doesn't depend on either high or low expectations. What was learned from the research wasn't what they thought they would learn. Funny how that some of the most important things you learn while you are busy working and seeking to learn something else.

Actually, at this point I realize that using this approach also dovetails with what I know about from the Bible about how we are encouraged to treat our relationship with God. By doing this with our relationship with God we are guaranteed to become blessed. It is what God got angry with the Hebrew people for not doing. I used to wonder how come God was so angry with them for disobeying what they had been told. From my perspective today it never was about that. God knew that the people would be more protected by and blessed if they took the attitude starting with the fact that God wanted good for them and to interpret everything in line with that fact. That attitude guarantees that we will be blessed because it builds it in with anticipation, and a perspective that allows for unending blessings to come to us.

When the Hebrew people got to the Promised Land they sent in 12 spies to scout the land. When they returned 10 spies who went into the Promised Land first and reported that the people who lived there were giants and that Israel would not be able to ever defeat them even though God had said the land was theirs. Those people were not beginning with the assumption that God wanted good for them. They operated from the position that they needed to believe what they saw and began with a position they believed even from their state of fear.

Two of the 12 who went into the land and said it was filled with milk and honey and that with God on their side they would be fine. Those two were interpreting everything from a perspective that God wanted good for them. They were ultimately blessed. It is a mindset that provides us with protection, blessings and a perspective that is more safe because it allows us to discern truth from falsehood, more easily. It is the perspective that because it is chosen grants more ability and flexibility because it affirms our choice. Just the other day I saw confirmation of this having to do with longevity. The more that a person reaches out with love toward others the more likely they are to live a long life. It is taking the position that is offered here. It is what you were doing when you were in love. You did it naturally.

What you were doing useful is that you were acting upon the belief, urge, emotion or course that seeing things in a positive way was a good thing. It felt good, helped you and became a motor for driving you into more love.

Now the really helpful ideas that the study pointed to were about how the couples treated each other when they were in love and the way they treated each other when they stayed in love.

The first one is something every therapist knows. The first thing to go in a troubled relationship when things get sour is this and it is the best first thing to add back into a relationship. That is the little things you do that say you are thinking of the other one. You know the little acts of kindness that say almost by themselves "Hey, I like you" See this act is a concrete example of how I think of you when you are not here. Things like cleaning and or fixing things when you are not around is a way of my saying I think of you and want good for you even when you are not here. When I do little things like bring you coffee, make your bed, or clean your car, I am saying I love you. Some folks leave notes and positive words while others leave a trail of helping acts of kindness and caring. Still others touch to show they are caring. Touch is very important and probably could be included to say you love your partner. Touching in ways that say to someone they are loved is more difficult than it may seem.

When you were in love you did these things or your versions of them without thinking about them. Unfortunately, when things began to get hectic this was one of the first things to go. It wasn't a comment as much about the relationship as it was about how busy and preoccupied you both were. Probably neither of you thought about the impact of not doing these small things for the other. But you can think of the positive effects of putting those things back into the relationship. If you begin to do them your partner may not notice right away, or they may not say anything right away, because of their skepticism, doubt, or fear, but if you keep it up they will notice and probably begin changing some of their behaviors as well, especially if you keep them secret and to yourself. Why keep them secret you might ask? It alters how you think and subtly alters your partner's thinking.

Now part of what you were doing right was allowing the mood to take you and to carry you forward. What stopped happening is the mood. Without active thought and actions no mood will sustain. It is the intentional act of evoking, sustaining and maintaining emotions that makes a difference. Who in our culture was going to tell you that, and yet therapist know this and so too do lots of folks. However, it wasn't going to be something that you would have learned, heard, or had pointed out to you. We usually learn it first the hard way, or can learn it most easily after we haven't acted upon it for a while. In the absence of acting upon this positive way we can see it much more clearly.

Even if someone told you that it was important what you dwell on to produce a particular emotion what would you have dwelled on to evoke that feeling of being in love?.............. Lots of folks have tried to do this and few have succeeded because of how they were thinking about what it means. It isn't something that follows logic and is easily done. It can be easily done but only when you know the secrets. They are coming.

Love Trance:

Because of what you did naturally it will be easier to get you back doing things by utilizing what you did that worked. It will also be easier to do when we offer some rules for maintaining your relationship that will actually help, and are doable. However, let's look at those things next chapter. This round let's focus on a practical approach that you were doing right.

When you were in love you probably did it all right, and if you didn't your partner covered for you in such a way that it kept working well. That is part of the success you two have is that when things were going well you both covered for the other and chalked it up to being glad you could help out.

A practical way of thinking about what you were doing right was that you were in a positive trance where you saw lots of options but you chose the ones that would further your relationship the most. You were focused on the relationship first and not your fear, ego, pride, etc. You were getting from giving and you were glad to be able to give. It was a great time for you. You were learning about yourself and you were enjoying doing things for your partner and you were taking credit for anything you did. You were pleased with yourself and with your relationship.

Let's face it another thing that you were doing was feeling great! It feels wonderful to be in love. It is exciting to learn about your partner. It is great just getting to be with them. If the truth were known it is exciting being able to do things for your partner. You were enjoying yourself, and you were anticipating the future, in whatever practical and useful way that you protected your feelings. Because you anticipated your partner liking you and continuing to like you in part because you liked them, things were great. It can be like that again. Yes, even if you have known each other for a long time especially if you are willing to begin discovering who they are each day, provided of course that they are a person you still want to be with.

Have you ever considered how difficult it is to keep yourself believing in yourself? It takes a lot of energy to keep believing in ourselves especially when things don't always go right. Besides most of us are our own worst enemies and are more critical of ourselves than anyone else. The good news is that you don't have to you can believe in something outside of yourself. People do it all the time. Some believe in teaching, some believe in medicine. Some people believe in the arts, some in sports. Some believe in God, and the good that we can do in God's name. It actually guarantees that you will feel good and also find positive meaning in what you do and are.

Of course it is also what we are encouraged to do in the Bible as well. Not only do our good deeds for others help them and us, it sets up a positive wave of behavior as well. The more we believe in ideas, things, and causes or even in doing good for others we can feel good about ourselves.

The story goes that a man who was traveling with a colleague was practicing this type of positive treatment of the world and was discovered by his colleague. The men were in a taxi and during lulls in their conversation the first man kept asking questions of the taxi driver and giving him compliments about what he knew and how well the taxi driver was driving. The second man just took it in and kept quiet. Yet, part of the second man's contribution to the conversation was how negative the city was and how hurtful and cold the people were in this big city.

After they both got out of the car the first one gave another compliment about how safe the taxi driver was and gave him a tip. As the taxi drove off the second man said, what were you doing? You know how negative the city is and yet you were chatting up that taxi driver and giving him compliments. What is up with that?

The first man said, Yes, you are right the city is very negative. That taxi driver was also somewhat depressed. He however was feeling better about himself after he dropped us off. He has probably another 8 customers he will pick up today. The mood he is in is a good one and if he causes 8 other people to be in better moods and to treat others better as well and even some of those people do the same there will be an explosion of good feelings and good deeds done today. The second man was quiet and thinking about the truth of what he just witnessed.

"A loving heart is the truest wisdom." - <u>Charles Dickens</u>

CHAPTER 7
WHAT ELSE THE STUDY SAID

The study said that couples who stayed in love did three things. They did small things for each other, and they interpreted what their partner said as positive and loving toward them and then responded as if it was true. Those three things seem so simple and yet they are profound. I will attempt to show how profound they are so that you can appreciate them more. However, putting them into practice requires some effort. Now, that is of course easier said than done, but it is easier than we might think especially when we look more closely at language.

First, since we recognize that 93% of communication is in our head, and comes from how we decide to interpret what it is that is said to us then we are primarily responsible for taking the conversation to either a loving or not so loving direction even if we don't realize that is in our power or even in our ability. I know that is a stretch to grasp that because only 7% of communication is words the rest is context, tone, and all the rest then it stands to reason that 93% of communication is actually what we think it is and that comes from our projections, fears, hopes, and attitudes. It is a radical idea that reality is something that we mostly make up because of the way we choose to see things. It is more than that. The way others treat us is mostly dependent upon how we interpreted their words to us, because most of the feedback they have from us is in the form of our responses to them.

Let's take a look at some statements that can be understood in a lot of different ways.

Carol: "Honey will you stop and pick up some milk on the way home?"

Bob has lots of possibilities he can chose. If he feels pressed and under pressure he may understand this as if she is saying, "He has nothing important to keep up with so any extra chore he should do." If so his response might be not so pleasant. All it would take is an angry "When do you think I am going to be able to do that?" and we would not be going to a good place.

If however he is feeling great because of the compliments he got at work, or last night from Carol he could hear it all together different. He could hear instead, as " Carol loves me so much she likes it when I participate in helping out and will appreciate my getting the milk. " It can be a chance to out do her and get her some flowers while I am at the grocery. Obviously, that one would be a lot different and taking the message to an entirely different place.

He could understand the sentence in at least 10 different ways that would range from negative to positive. Some would be more neutral, others would be more positive and others more negative. His response no matter how he interprets it makes a difference for the relationship. While we all think that we know exactly what something means when we are spoken to a lot of how it can be understood is entirely in our head, and up to us. Let's say that he realizes he is in a bad mood and decides to shield Carol from a negative thought, and so he reasons that he is a little suspicious that instead of responding to her critical comment he responds as if she was being loving to him. We still then are going to go into a positive place because then when he gets to see her positive response to his he can know she was being positive with him all along and it was his fear.

Now let's take it one further. Let's say that Bob believes in his heart Carol was being critical of what he had to do, and still he decides to respond to her as if she loves him with a comment that implies he knows that and that he loves her. Something like, "Carol I know you think I am superman and that is wonderful, knowing that you think so highly of me. I believe in you as well. I will of course get the milk even though it has been a difficult day even for superman." Bob in responding this way is still taking the relationship down a good path to a good place. He is choosing to respond to Carol's doubt with such a positive spin that she is going to probably like it as well. I believe he is doing here what he would have done more naturally if he was back in love. His comments communicate that he is in love with her at this point and she could feel it, if she chooses too.

The point is that almost every interaction is filled with that much ambiguity. Even if Carol's voice is strained and angry when she asks, because of past miscommunications, or because of how bad the traffic is at the time or because of how she is in pain from a headache, Bob can choose how to respond to her. It is completely in his ability to choose. Just like all of us. However, our culture hasn't made it clear that so much of what we think and react to is entirely in our head and up to how we choose to interpret it.

There are some things that can get in our way. Often those are beliefs that are not so useful. But we got them somewhere and they need to be dealt with one way or another. Some of those things come from our culture and some are just bad habits that have gotten picked up.

Frequently we think our partner needs to respond to us in a certain way before we can say, do, feel or have the intimacy we are wanting with them. The rules we have for ourselves that way are amazing. We might think that he/she has to understand where I am coming from, or agree with me, or have initiated some actions that I can respond to before we can have an intimate moment. I am not sure where we would have gotten that message but it's similar to the one that many of us have that challenges this whole approach. It implies that we have to respond to any message we are given in the tone and style that we think it is sent to us. Many folks have the idea that they are not allowed to be more creative with their answers. It is as if they are under some strict edict that says they must respond to what they interpret to be the question.

Sometimes though many of us have felt that we were only able to respond to what was said, and we hoped our partner was going to say or do a certain thing so that we could have that perfect intimate experience. Unfortunately, our partner may not have gotten the script. When we were tied to only responding to what was said in some strict way we were stuck. It doesn't matter if they didn't get the script. We can make it up if what we are wanting is a good relationship. You did that naturally when you were in love. That is what the study showed. When you were in love you spontaneously chose the positive way to understand what your partner said and you then replied in an equally positive way.

If all we were doing was simply responding to words it would be profound enough but this goes beyond words and impacts emotions and how you will feel the rest of the day and your life. No this isn't Pollyanna; this is actually about neuroscience and language. It is about understanding that much of our life is spent in trances of one type or another and that those are either going to be chosen or happen by happen stance. It is about acknowledging how much our choices impact our reality and our experiences.

The emotions that you feel in the presence of your partner will have a tendency to impact him/her as well. Your feeling of love that is communicated in your tone of voice even in something as benign as, "Please pass the toast", tends to have an impact on your partner. Your positive emotions and positive responses elicit a similar positive response. It is well documented in neuroscience and is referred to as mirroring neurons. It means that in your presence I am likely to begin to feel what you are feeling especially if you are feeling it very powerfully.

We have known for a very long time that feelings can be passed. What we didn't know is that they can be passed so powerfully. What we also haven't known well is how to change what we feel. Yet, that is exactly what this approach is about, because emotions often come from trances that we spontaneously find ourselves in. We can also alter those trances and invite different emotions. While we know that emotions can be passed between people it stands to reason that the emotions can be passed very easily between people who you care about and who care about you.

Among experienced therapists who deal with trance the common understanding is that sometimes our clients can trance us into seeing the world through their perspective. It is both a good thing and a not so good thing. Marriage and Family Therapists sometimes refer to this as joining. A therapist intentionally might join with a family so that he/she might be able to understand the family better and to become more able to impact it once they understand it viscerally. It can be a bad thing when we don't know how to get out of feeling what we started feeling in their presence.

The way a person would know whether the emotion they were feeling was from the person they were with or their own would come by knowing themselves and how they were feeling before the other person came into the room. If you were feeling calm and pleasant and when your friend came into the room you started to feel scared, hurt or angry you would then know where you got the feelings. Letting them go temporarily is a trance shift and you can do it by imagining the emotions passing right out of you. Alas, it is only a temporary fix.

The concept of passing emotions is so profound that the Bible tells us to guard ourselves against people who are angry. Their anger can infect us with their world view and cause similar flares of anger to theirs that are not helpful. We are however encouraged to be around people who are willing to grow, learn, and delight in being thankful, appreciative, and grateful. By being that ourselves we impact our life and will actually, impact the people we come into contact with whether they realize it or not. Your good mood can and will impact others just through your regular daily interactions. The more you fill up with a positive feeling and then interact the more positive impact your words will have.

In formal hypnotic trance a hypnotist might want to help their client to know they are in a trance and have some concrete example of being in a trance so they could use the experience more powerfully. Hypnotists know that trances are so common that to really believe you are in a different trance you might need something to convince you that it is real. The term referring to this is "ratify". A good hypnotist might build in an experience for a client to help them ratify the fact that they were in a trance. If your hypnotist has one of your arms floating out in front of you and you didn't really raise it there it seems as if it is a ratification that you are or were in a trance. The same would be true if you felt your whole emotional side becoming more and more hopeful, or bright.

In a certain sense the comment and emotion we put to a response does that in a non-hypnotic way every time we speak with our partner. We ratify for our partner whether they can think of our response as a positive one or a hurtful one. It allows us to direct them toward being in and feeling in Love. So every response we have in a certain way ratifies for our partner that we think they love us and that we love them. It becomes a way that the both of you can contribute to the "in Love"

When you were prompted by feeling in Love you did this naturally and repeatedly. It is just as effective and more lasting to do intentionally and knowingly to create for yourself and your partner a sense of being in love that you can sustain indefinably.

One way to do it is by intentionally allowing you to have those positive emotions and simply ask for or say something so natural that it would be something said 1000's of times. You just might be surprised by the response that you get. The emotion you convey just might surprise you from the response you get. The emotion that you feel strongly toward your partner can electrify the air between you and your partner. Ok so if you don't get any response you can keep at it and notice what happens. It might just teach you a profound lesson. It has others.

So what happens when you are suddenly unhappy with your partner's responses and or reaction to you? The good news is you can do something about this. The bad news is that the issue is probably yours. No, we aren't going to blame you or your partner. Your feelings are simply the result of what you tell yourself and how you interpret his/

her responses to you. No, that doesn't make you responsible for them. It simply means you get to be responsible for your feelings. Actually, that is good news, and the idea comes from Cognitive Behavioral Therapy and is well documented.

Consider that it is your feelings, and your sense of unhappiness that is the issue. If your partner simply doesn't like you or is rejecting you that is one thing, but almost any other issue that is about your feeling is about you. The really good news about this approach is the following. That if your partner was really rejecting you and not taking responsibility for it your using this approach will free you to better see that and allow you to also be in a more safe mindset to deal with whatever you discover, because you will be using all of your resources instead of only some of them.

When someone is not using all their resources and they are acting upon their fears or hurts then some characteristic unpleasant things can occur. It reminds me of how that one woman was so upset with her husband because he didn't realize she was hurt. I asked her if she had told her husband how come she was upset. She looked shocked and said, "NO," in an emphatic voice. "He should know how come I am upset." She actually, believed that even though he was/is male he should simply know because it was so obvious to his wife the reason she was upset. That he didn't know was proof that he didn't love her in her mind. She was certain that his inaction meant that he didn't love her.

I was so shocked by her comments because at first I didn't believe she was serious. She was. She meant every word she said. It was the world that she lived in. It took her a while to realize that everyone didn't know what she knew, and that for her husband to know some of the things she wanted him to know she would have to tell him. Those types of illogical beliefs about relationships and people that we live with can make a difference that block us from being who we can be with our partner and with ourselves. The belief the above woman had wasn't going to get better, until she examined it. She couldn't do that until she realized that it wasn't helping her and that believing someone should know something because it is obvious to you doesn't help.

Most of the things that get into our way about relationships are like that. They came from assumptions, beliefs, and experiences that we had in one way or another that contributed to our overall beliefs about couples and how they should and can act.

The historic things that get in the way most of us realize come from the relationships we have had and from our fears. What we don't often realize is that those historic things can change for us by how we chose to see things today. How we continue to interpret events from our past changes how our past effects us and affects us. It works through the means of trance. When a person focuses on the negative it means then that everything will be colored by the negative feelings and the negative experiences. When we rewrite our history by focusing on a different aspect we can get an entirely different picture and different feeling about ourselves and our past. We in effect are literally rewriting our history. This isn't a dishonest thing it is all about focus. In fact, it happens all the time whether we realize it or not. Memory is altered by decisions we are making about today and our future. It isn't a digital recording it is fluid and always changing. We might as well make use of it instead of being victims of it. When you were in love you rewrote events of a day so that things that were not as wonderful as you would like became background and the things that were great became the focus of your attention. In some ways it literally changes the past. It doesn't negate what happened but it changes the way it impacts us and what wisdom it can offer us.

One young woman recently decided to take me seriously about this concept and do something about her relationship with her father. Her parents had divorced when she was a young girl and she had gotten into a habit of remembering and focusing mostly on the negative things that had occurred. She decided to stop that and to rewrite her history so to speak by focusing on the good things that she hadn't been allowing herself to do. She said she cried for a long time when she realized how many positive things she had been overlooking. She didn't deliberately distort her history either time. She had both times simply focused on certain aspects of her relationship and as a result found the folder of all the things like that in her memory. When she opened the other folder or way of thinking about her father an entirely different perspective came about. She is a very wise young woman. When she realized how helpful this was in altering her relationship with her father she decided to do a similar thing with her own past.

One couple I recently saw were struggling with being together in part because they both believed they should spend all their free time together. Since, both of them were independent types of people that wasn't working well and they snarled at each other and were unhappy that things were not working the way they believed they should. When they realized that it was not only ok, to have some alone time it probably would keep their relationship healthy and alive, especially since, they were both a little bit of introverts. Introverts can better charge their batteries alone than together. The couple is much happier with each other at this point. And yes, they are in Love.

"Whoso loves believes the impossible." - Elizabeth Barrett Browning

CHAPTER 8
SPONTANEOUSLY THINKING POSITIVE THOUGHTS ABOUT EACH OTHER

Ok, by now you realize it isn't as easy as just deciding to do it. You may even have discovered that it can be actually difficult to think of positive things especially when you are in a certain mood, or your partner has a certain mood, or face that seems to push every button you have so that you discovered irritations, hurts, fears, and unpleasant thoughts. Good! Now we are ready to get down to actually putting this into practice. We pretty much had to get to this point before we could put it into practice. If you had not tried and discovered that it isn't as easy as it sounds it would be even more difficult. It isn't easy unless you know the secrets. Knowing yourself and what bothers you helps.

First, deciding to think positively about someone takes personal risk and requires courage as well as an effort. It pays off but it isn't something that just anyone can do easily. Anyone can criticize, but not everyone can think of positive things to say that are honest. That is the one and only absolute. Whatever positive thing that you say must be true. Here is the first lesson about this. There is a lot of room to grow about what constitutes true for most of us when we are thinking about positive things. It usually involves learning to be diplomatic and being able to focus on what you do like and ignoring what you don't like for the immediate time. It also involves realizing that truth doesn't always mean telling all that you have thought. You wouldn't any other time or with anyone else how come we have thought that it was any different with our partner. They and we both deserve to have a filter that blocks random thoughts from being expressed. Very few of us have thoughts so pure that all of them could be expressed!

The average person thinks first of some critical thing or just a state of criticism. They can even proclaim their criticism as true. They can also struggle to believe as true some positive thing that came as a second thought. Yet, does it make something more true that you thought of it first? Does it make something more true if it is critical? Lots of folks believe so. They live their lives that way and actually believe that if something is critical they must believe it more. That position only gives false hope to the person wanting to be honest. It is an admirable position to take so that we won't fool ourselves but it isn't true. In fact, it perpetuates unpleasant beliefs as true and robs us of what can be.

Whether something is hurtful, critical or unkind doesn't make it true. Neither does accessing a critical and negative perspective make anything true. Actually, a very good case could be made that thinking positive about others is much more likely to be true because they are always wanting to do and be seen positively by others. Even most criminals aren't really seeking to harm as much as they are seeking to do something good for themselves. It doesn't make sense to so widely accuse others of being intentionally hurtful. Actually taking that stance makes us more vulnerable to being manipulated. Most manipulation isn't done in an intentional fashion it is done because that is something that has worked for a long time and so it is done almost automatically.

Consider that few of us dress up so that others will criticize us. I don't know anyone who wants others to dislike them. I know people who have said they did, but they were not being completely honest. They wanted people to like them so much that they were trying to not be so vulnerable. We all want others to like us and usually even when we mess up we want others to give us the benefit of the doubt and assume we meant well. When we treat others like that and assume and ascribe positive motives and intentions to their actions, we are treating them the way we would like to be treated.

Often though we have trouble hearing what the other person has said in a positive way when we are so aware of our own hurt that we have trouble moving to a positive place. So the first thing is to realize any difficulty in thinking of positive things is ours. It isn't about our partner. It isn't about our own mindset. It is our bias and our difficulty in being able to attribute positive things to others especially when we are hurting, scared, or defensive. It is about where and about what we have spent our time being able to do. After some practice you can and will be more able to do it and it will have a major impact on you, because it won't simply impact how you relate with your partner but also with yourself.

So, asking ourselves how come it is so difficult for us is a good place to begin. It means that we begin with what can become a great learning place for us. There are all sorts of reasons that we could attribute but here is the thing. If you are willing to simply learn and continue learning no matter what then it won't even matter what was the old reason because it can become changed.

One way is to ask yourself what someone else could attribute positively to your partner when you had difficulty thinking of some positive motive. Another way that I believe is easier is to begin with a belief. When you begin there it is easier. I know that my partner wants good for me so what is the good that she/he wants? By beginning with the belief that your partner wants good for you makes responding in a positive way much easier. .

A second way that helps me with others is to understand where they are coming from. A man who said some very unpleasant things to someone who I care about is also a person I have to interact with on occasion. At first, I was so angry and righteously morally judgmental about what he said that he shouldn't have that I couldn't see how come he was so hurt that he blurted out things he shouldn't have. I was hurt and someone I care about was hurt and I wanted revenge, or something like it. I wanted satisfaction. I wanted him to not be able to say those types of things. Because of being somewhat creative I thought of lots of ways to get even. I also thought about this scene a lot, until I realized that my thoughts were not helping.

After praying that I would be able to think of a way to get beyond this without some major upheaval, I waited. After a while it came to me that my anger wasn't helping anything and that I could let go of it. So I did. Actually, I remembered a quote that helped me a lot. The quote is this, "Your anger does not bring about the righteousness of God", It made me realize I could let go of the anger and discover another way.

When I reflected back on who he really is and what I know about him and who he wants people to think he is I got a very different picture, than the one of his being so foolish and immature that I had before. While today he is healthy looking and seems strong. He is hurting in so many ways and has so few options open to him because of sickness, and the lasting effects of sickness that he is pretty frustrated. Although he works every day and looks healthy enough today, he had a very serious round of illness a few years back that left him a broken man. He has few options because of insurance premiums. He has few options left from what the illness took from him financially, relationally, and professionally. If there is a recipe for creating a negative trance that would be it. Feeling frustrated and without many options it would be difficult to see the options that would be easy for me to see in my current situation. When it occurred to me where he was coming from I realized that forgiving him was the only thing that made sense. It didn't matter that he might think I was excusing his behavior. It was easy and you know what? He was very appreciative. He grinned like someone had given him back a shiny new present. He was embarrassed about where he was and what he had said. He was also so hurt and embarrassed that he didn't have enough ego to say so. His reaction seemed very plain to me. I am glad that I treated him as if he wanted to be a good and decent person. It solved a real dilemma for me.

It would have been easy to have remained angry with him and blamed him. He was wrong and there was no question about it. However, it wouldn't have helped him, nor me. It points to another truism. Usually when we are having difficulties with someone a good place to start is with what we are assuming they are capable of or that they know. More arguments that I ever had at the prison where I was the chaplain for so long were because I assumed someone was more capable than they did. It became almost a first step for me. When someone was arguing with me for something that didn't make sense I would begin to consider what way had I overestimated her ability that she felt accused about or criticized about. Often their estimate of what they were capable of was much less than mine and theirs trumped mine in the argument, because their disbelief in themselves would distort positive message I said especially if it was mostly just factual. Usually, I might overlook how hurt they were because of how angry or competent they were to argue. That one almost always meant an argument. But also when I would over estimate someone's capabilities they took my overestimate of their ability as an insult. They were right to, because overestimating someone's capabilities implies we didn't really notice them, and their fear. It also doesn't give them credit for what they have achieved. Besides it tends to cause them fear of not living up to our standard. Lots of folks besides me are guilty of this besides me and they usually, like I did, mean well. It is just that when our estimate is so above where they think they can achieve the usual person doesn't experience the compliment but the fear, hurt and aloneness of not being understood or recognized as who they believe themselves to be.

One woman who I gave a copy of my book about dealing with manipulation to, proved this in a glaring way. She came back and said ok, but what was she to do? I told her to use the techniques that were listed under the section on power struggles. She got quiet and frustrated and said, with tears streaming down her face. I don't understand the book. I tried to read it but it doesn't make any sense to me. She said, I read Daniel Steel novels and have to skip a lot of the words because I don't know them. I don't understand what you were saying, and now I feel dumb and stupid as well. When she said this I felt convicted of making a terrible mistake that hurt her and was a senseless mistake. The book is written at the 12 grade level, and is difficult for someone who reads at more of a 6th grade ability. I never meant for anything like that to happen. The book was written while I was working on my doctorate and reading doctorate level books. I taught her other techniques, but she taught me a very important lesson.

She taught me a lesson that was important for me to learn. I will always be in her debt. I never meant to make her feel stupid. I wanted her to feel empowered. I wanted her to be able to recognize she had options. It was never my intent to hurt her or to make her feel less than. I want to rewrite the book so it will be more useful to others. It needs it badly.

It isn't just overestimating someone's reading ability or even intelligence that I am talking about. When we overestimate someone's ability in a certain area it can bring a similar response. Not many of us are truly renaissance people able to do all things well. Even if we are very competent in one thing we may not feel competent in another area. Our feelings of incompetence can distort how we hear anything in that subject.

It is my hope that by discussing these types of things you are reminded of times that you have done similar things. I suspect that you understand and can relate either on one side or the other. Having been on both sides of the situation makes it a lot easier to understand and take care of the miscommunication that could ensue.

Dwelling on or reminding ourselves of how often we have been wrong in the past or misread something helps but it isn't the best way. It however can help because it reminds us that our tendency is to see things that are regular and habitual in our eyes not that others will see them that way as well.

One rule I have for myself has to do with my relationship with my wife. It is that I do my best to not read her with my intuition about anything having to do with me. There really is a practical reason that it is very good for us to never use our intuition or at least seldom with our partner. It is that with them no matter how good we might be with others we probably will get it wrong often enough to cause difficulties. The reason is that they matter too much. Even a professional gambler knows that needing something too much makes us not make good decisions. When it comes to reading people no matter how good we are with others it is a good idea to turn it off with our partner. The people who have believed me about this and stopped have been very glad they did.

Turning off our reading of another person is an intentional act that requires more than a little bit of intentionality and a willingness to be vulnerable on the one hand. On the other it means that we rely on a different way of keeping ourselves safe. We rely on asking the other person questions so we know what is going on, and we refrain from making quick decisions. It is a calming approach

An example from a couple I saw a while back. Both Brenda and Carl had grown up in rough circumstances. They had used their wits about them to be ok, and they got very good at reading people. They both had jobs where their ability to read people helped them and they were relatively successful at their respective careers. When they came to me they were not getting along well at all. He was so hurt by her comments, and she was so afraid and hurt by his behavior that she was ready for him to leave. She was/ is a very intense introvert and he is more than a little of an extravert. Between the two of them reading the others mood and not checking things out with each other they were at loggerheads. They were frustrating themselves and getting no where. Until introverts and extroverts understand their differences they can misunderstand what each needs as a rejection. When they understand how each other work and what they need they can be a great help to each other, because there are benefits from both styles of thinking.

He was an extrovert and kept offering to her opportunities to be with people. She frequently turned him down and although she explained how come he only felt rejected. Because he interpreted her need to be alone as a rejection he would then respond in kind and they were then arguing a lot.

An introvert will enjoy people but will need time alone to recharge. They will also think through what they are going to say sometimes deeply. Often they haven't appreciated how useful their style of thinking is to themselves and others because they have believed that extroverts were more important.

Extroverts may enjoy being alone as well but they recharge their batteries from being with other people. Unless some introvert helps them to understand that everyone doesn't get energy from parties and being with people they think they do and are gleefully offering to everyone what helps them.

When I first noticed how much they both read me I knew that they were probably over doing it with each other. I could tell that they were both watching me very closely and interpreting how they understood my facial expressions, my body movements and my tone of voice. They were assessing what they saw and making judgments based heavily on what they interpreted rather than on what was said. When I told them about my rule for self and how come I use it. They understood. When we began to talk about the hurt they both realized they were completely missing what was up with the other person. They had externalized their fear and were projecting what they were afraid the other one thought. As a result they were pleasantly surprised that what both had been afraid of wasn't even in or near reality. She was afraid he was rejecting her because of the time she spent with the kids. He just knew that she was rejecting him because she spent time in her office at home alone. Besides, she kept saying that she needed some alone time. He thought that meant she didn't like him. When they both realized that they were misunderstanding what the other was saying they had an entirely different situation. Actually, they then began to be able to feel in Love and to treat each other as if what the other said was from a loving place. They did very well. They did so in part because with new information they were able to understand each other in a new light that wasn't rejecting them. They also were more able to hear the others requests. They had returned to how they treated each other when they were in love. By returning to that loving position they were able to keep it going because now they had some new tools to do that. They also had the major way they had miss-communicated out of the way. They were free to simply be in love and to relate with affection. When I last saw them they were working together as a team appreciating each other.

"Love is the only sane and satisfactory answer to the problem of human existence." - Erich Fromm

CHAPTER 9
DOING IT WILL BE LIKE LEARNING TO RIDE A BIKE

It is scary to think that we get to choose how to understand reality. It takes a while to overcome the cultural dishonesty that occurs and most of us pick up like toxic air. We are mostly indoctrinated to believe that what we see is reality. We are not really taught to recognize that how we see something depends on what learning we have and what we have thought before hand. It is pretty easy to understand that for most things "what we see is what we get" works well. It however is also a very different thing when someone studies how inaccurate eye witness's testimony actually is when tested. It becomes even more clear when we start to understand how fluid memory is as well. But we are led to believe that memory is or can be very accurate. That is somewhat true in tests of memory where there is nothing to corrupt the memory but when we have a vested interest to see something a certain way it alters how we see it and what we can see. If we have a strong emotion connected to the memory that can easily distort what we remember.

For instance, when one spouse is cheating on the marriage, the other spouse doesn't recognize what is happening. Everyone else may recognize that the cheater is cheating, but the non cheating spouse may have a difficult time seeing that. However, when the cheating comes to light, and they are sorry for their actions and wanting to change another phoneme begins. Now the spouse who didn't see it before now sees signs of cheating everywhere. They are so suspicious that they see signs where there are none. That doesn't mean they should distrust their fears but it does mean their intuition took a hit when they found out the affair was going on in the first place, and it isn't going to be healed just because the truth now is known.

In fact, the affair may well be over but being able to see that might take some effort, and the objective eyes and understanding of a therapist to assist sorting the wheat from chaff. When our trust in our intuition has been so damaged by some event like our overlooking an affair it is going to take a while for us to overcome the issue. I suggest to people that they first realize the hurt that has occurred and to also forgive themselves for not seeing what they didn't see. Secondly, I would suggest that we take some time to regain trust in our intuition. Part of the way of doing that is by allowing your intuition to tell you things and then check them out. After a while you will again be feeling confident of your intuitive ability.

It is likely that the closeness you have with a spouse is what caused the inability to see what was going on. Lots of folks want to blame the non-offending spouse. Some therapists inadvertently blame by suggesting that they have some reason to not see. Before it was brought to my attention I have implied that the person didn't want to see it. Implying that blames the non- offending spouse. I believe that the real reason is that the closer we are to someone the more distorted our intuition about them will be. It actually doesn't imply something negative about the non-offending spouse but something good. He/

she is capable of being deeply caring and involved in the relationship to a deep level. The reason that we can be tricked about affairs is the same reason that we shouldn't trust our intuition about day to day events with our spouse. Our perceptions can be altered by our emotions.

The best way to keep from having major misunderstandings between spouses who read each other is to simply stop acting upon our intuition with our spouse and ask questions so that we are not inadvertently jumping to conclusions.

To go a little farther with how memory and perception are impacted by our histories let's talk about perception and how we interpret things we see and understand. Surely you have had times when you realized that your feelings clouded what you could and could not see. Two people who are seeing the same action of government can declare it to be two very different things if they have opposing views. Someone from the far right is going to see the same actions very differently than someone from the far left. Both will be certain they are right. Both will be almost incensed that the other even sees what they see. They may label their opponent's views as juvenile, ignorant, stupid, or naïve.

So how can we choose to believe a certain view over what we automatically tend to see? What we have been taught to see in this culture is what is wrong. We have been taught how to find the flaw, and complain. We have been taught how to criticize others. We have been taught to have a knee jerk reaction of criticism, especially if we feel a certain thing. We have especially been taught to believe our feelings, and our first reactions. Unfortunately, our first reactions often demonstrate more about what we have been thinking and what we are accustomed to seeing than what others who might be objective would see. Choosing to see a certain thing actually allows us to more deeply know the truth than any amount of criticism.

Being critical sounding can make even something foolish sound accurate. It can sound authoritative and it can even sound true. Lies told with criticism, and an authoritative air are usually more believable. Inmates in prison do it all the time. It doesn't make them true. Besides if we are critical and waiting for our partner to somehow become amazingly positive toward us while we continue to be critical, skeptical, and even belittling it is even less likely to happen than the winning lottery ticket will blow into my yard and I will pick it up. What is amazing to me is that even though we can all recognize the truth of this, we don't. It is often only when we have been in a trance of being hurt that we think in those ways, toward our partner, and still expect them to respond to us with kindness and patience. Only someone in a negative trance could expect that they could get back sweetness and love from the person they offer anger, blaming and criticism.

Moving beyond the affair, or anger and intuition to how to implement the approach that is offered here we get to a very different place because we begin by deciding how to respond to our partner even before they are going to speak. It takes a personal responsibility for our contribution to the communication at the emotional level. It is a decision to do this and it has to do with our willingness to shape reality and be responsible for the reality that we are co-creating with our partner. It means giving them the benefit of the doubt and that probably isn't going to happen easily after an affair, or betrayal of some sort. When that is over and you can again offer some positive response then we are ready to begin again taking responsibility for our being in love again.

However deciding to be taking responsibility for our side of the communication and actually attribute a positive message to what is said to us gives the possibility that it could be true. It usually is. People who like us want to say positive things to us and even when they don't they still want to be seen in a positive light. Being able to see it and label it that way takes some time to do just like it did when you learned to ride a bike. It is way more useful and especially more fun to do because it can take you places the bike could not.

Actually, attempting to do this takes some courage and it takes a willingness to realize that reality is what each of us live in that we created in our heads. It came from the stuff we got from our culture and our beliefs, fears, experiences and hopes. It takes a while to really digest that concept that we live in the reality that we chose, because it is dependent on how we see things and chose to see things. Yet, that concept is so foreign to our culture that it is more than a little bit difficult to swallow. However, wouldn't it be better to live in a reality that we wanted and that our hopes, and desires created, than one that our fears and disappointments created? You either get to choose the reality you live in or your fears choose it for you.

For instance most folks believe that we are supposed to answer a question that is asked of us, or if not we should state that we are not going to answer the question. Any question can be understood on many different levels we can choose which level we would answer the question. We can also choose what level of positive response we want to acknowledge. For instance, the following illustration shows how insistent we can become about assuming good and excluding the negative meaning.

Diane: {In an angry voice,} Why are you still doing the job you are doing, why haven't you gotten a promotion?
David: Wow! You really care about me, so much you believe I deserve a promotion. I sure wish everyone believed in me. Thanks I love you too.

David didn't comment on or match the anger. He also didn't attempt to answer the question because there is no real answer to the question asked, as it was asked. However, I bet that Diane could appreciate that he was assuming she wanted good for him and not that she was attacking him. If she was responding to how frustrated she was about how David wasn't being recognized for his accomplishments then the assumption would be right. In a smaller context the two statements seem almost to not go together. If you laughed at the response then good. Whatever your response was it can teach you something about yourself and how willing you are to live with the rules that restrict how well we can relate to each other.

Just because someone has anger in their voice doesn't mean it is meant for us. Just because there isn't anger in a person's voice doesn't mean it isn't there for us either. Even if we know the anger is toward us doesn't mean that we have to address it, or respond to it. We can choose what and when we will respond. Part of learning that you can respond to what you want to and be responsible for what we say it is a good thing.

We have been conditioned to assume that we should respond to the attack or the implied insult, and neither are true. We can choose what and how we respond. We are not responsible for what is said to us only how and what we respond. Besides we only know what we interpreted the statement to be about. We don't really know what the intent was of the person speaking to us. Ok, so sometimes we do but that is not often the case with our partner unless we are assuming something positive.

When we respond a couple of rounds of this type of assumptions to someone who is angry they have a decision to make if their anger is at us in the first place. It might not have been and our responding to them in a positive way can have helped. If they were angry with us then are they going to confront us or switch to the more positive that we have adopted. If they confront us then it can go something like the following.

Diane: Why are you saying such positive things? I am angry with you and I want you to know that.
David: I am aware of your anger and I still believe you love me. If you are willing to tell me what you are angry about I am willing to hear it.

Here David isn't ignoring her or her anger, but what is implied in the air is that he will ignore anger that is not direct and said in such a way that it can be resolved. An indirect method may be a plea for more help in addressing something but it may be the person doesn't know how to say difficult things. By saying the positive we have now a situation where we can be positive and resolve the conflict if possible. By responding to the negative emotions and accusations the conversation would not be positive. The negative other way would have only resulted in a fight and only distance would have been achieved. During which time Diane may have been able to think of how to address what she was really upset about.

It feels awkward at first to assume that our partner is saying something good to us when they are criticizing us. It also feels awkward and almost untrue to respond to something that our spouse said as if we assume it to be positive. It can become very empowering and satisfying as well as helpful in avoiding arguments.

Besides it allows us to be the one making a decision to become closer and to alter the relationship in a positive way. It is about our personal choice and we have much more ability to do that than any of us may have really understood. Most of us really want our partner to like and believe in us. What we do is designed to elicit that respect.

Unfortunately, what got respect in my family may not get respect in your family. Besides, most of us believe another lie that our culture has perpetuated. It is this. Attention and affection are not as valuable if I have to ask. Nothing could be more foolish than that in relationships. It assumes that our partner knows how we feel, and think as well as we do. It also makes a foolish assumption about attention and affection being devalued because of asking for them. Actually, asking increases the likeliness that they will receive what they need, and that both parties will be happy.

Our culture has all sorts of rules that this approach is breaking. Some have to do with what reality is, while others seem to be more focused on boundaries, or things just happening instead of our being able to make them happen. Being in charge of whether you get your needs met and are able to be deeply in love is very empowering. It also brings about a powerful way that you can again evoke and reawaken your being in love.

"The three hardest tasks in the world are neither physical feats nor intellectual achievements, but moral acts: 1) To return love for hate; 2) To include the excluded; and 3) To say 'I was wrong.'"
- Ernst Heinrich Haeckel

CHAPTER 10
OK, SO NOW YOU HAVE HAD A POSITIVE EXPERIENCE

You realized it has some benefits and have seen it work. Your spouse may well have asked you what you were up to or how come you were being so positive. That would be a good thing and I hope that you told them you were making a change in how you want to live, or at least took full responsibility. If you didn't now would be a good time to do that and tell your spouse you are making a change and you hope it won't distress them too much. You may need to even tell them that you are going to be making other positive changes because you value them and your relationship with them so much you realize there are things you can do that can improve the relationship and how you relate.

You may also have seen that it worked well until you got angry, or hurt and responded out of your hurt in the moment. Of course when we are angry we don't tend to use all our resources. At times we are so emotionally invested and so hurt that we may not see what is right beside us. We can only see what is right in front.

In my thinking and the persistent focus on what was done to me that hurt me that would generate a negative trance and while in it we would seldom make good decisions. It is unlikely that we would say things that would lead to a good place for others as well. It is my hope that I can show a new way by demonstrating how to exit the negative trance.

When we find ourselves in a negative trance it is possible to go 180 degrees but it isn't possible or isn't for most people to move from a negative trance to no trance. Most folks can move from a negative one to a positive trance. One way is to openly acknowledge how we are feeling and to then add to that awareness by acknowledging other truths, or other awareness that is in a different sensory mode. So while I was angry to begin to switch I could become aware of the feel of the chair I am in and the sounds around me as well as truths of beliefs I have about myself that are foundational. By also acknowledging the fear that is a part of being hurt we can begin to change our feelings. Hurt and anger can slip into any and all of our secret fears. If we are afraid of being humiliated, or hurt with no way to defend ourselves from a bully then that is part of what goes through our mind. It may be very uncomfortable and it can also help us if we are willing to use it as a sign for us. In fact, the fear can become a wonderful detector of an area of our life that can be improved. Whatever we are afraid of we are not seeing our strength or we wouldn't be afraid. One wonderful thing about fear is that right next to it is a strength that we aren't paying attention to because of how loud the fear is to us. Yet, the only reason the fear is so loud is that we are not seeing the strength that is already there.

If you were to do this with any anger you would or could begin to feel better, very quickly. The reason is that it is very easy to move from where you are by noticing sensory items and then gradually moving to another trance that is in effect positive. It is simply accepting where we are with all the emotions that we are in fact having at the time, and then noticing other things around us, near us and then the emotion we would like to be evoking in ourselves. It doesn't happen by setting the hurt and fear of the anger aside it happens by facing them and acknowledging them as well as other things that I am aware of. It also happens because as we start to address our strengths and to become aware of how that through this we will become stronger and more in touch with how to cope with this situation better in the future. And it is true.

Making the shift from a negative trance to a positive one when we are feeling hurt or angry with our spouse may be easier than it is to change how we feel when someone does something to us that is very public and hurtful. What happens usually between us and a spouse is more private. It doesn't always hurt less but usually it doesn't have as many witnesses. For many of us the public hurt is either much easier or more difficult to deal with than private hurt. I suspect that the private hurt feels like it is a betrayal, and so it sometimes hurts more. Yet, other folks tend to experience public betrayal as more personal and hurtful. It depends upon how we think of each as to whether we would be bothered by it or not.

However, tomorrow I am about to see a couple who shamed each other publicly. There was an affair that was then told around as retaliation by the hurt one of the couple. Now the original hurt has been compounded by embarrassment. In getting revenge the originally hurt spouse has now hurt both of them even further. It is understandable. The usual couple does this same thing by telling their family and friends, and so it is common that this happens. When a partner is hurt they often tell their family and friends. When or if the hurt is resolved the family and friends take a lot longer to overlook the hurt because nothing was done to help them overcome the feelings they had about their loved one being hurt. It creates further problems for both parties. That doesn't mean we should keep silent and never tell. It does mean that telling before anything is done is not always a good idea.

Have you ever noticed how that we often want to hurt the other person until we stop hurting? It isn't all that useful of a desire but it is one that most of us have felt. Having the desire and acting upon it are two different things. To act upon the desire to get revenge often ends in our feeling bad about ourselves. Oh the end result is often so far removed from the act that we have lots of time in between that feels so sweet that we got that revenge, but ultimately it often isn't very sweet. Being able to forgive ourselves is usually more difficult than forgiving others. I am not sure if the hurt spouse spoken of above will be able to forgive him/herself in time to fix the relationship. It may well depend on how much he/she is willing to experience forgiveness for him/herself.

One major mistake we tend to make is thinking and acting as if our partner or the person who hurt us can make it better. Usually, once we are hurt it is ours. It is now something that we have to deal with and fix, because no matter how much we didn't want it the situation is that we are the one who has to fix it. Most folks rebel at that because they say it isn't fair. They didn't do anything to cause the hurt their spouse should fix it. That may be how a person feels but it has nothing to do with how things actually work.

One way of thinking about this was taught to me in a powerful way by a young man who was in an automobile wreck that left him a quadriplegic. He had been minding his own business and hadn't done anything wrong. Yet because of someone else he was now and would be forever in a wheel chair. He had no anger for the person who hit him. He simply accepted his situation as it was. Sounds difficult to believe but actually, it is the healthiest and most powerful way to get on with life and be able to salvage as much as possible. Staying angry simply continues the pain. I have known several people who were hurt so badly their lives were changed forever and they didn't harbor anger toward the person who caused them to be in the shape they were in. The young man who I was speaking about above is an incredible man. He is deeply spiritual and actually has a wonderful attitude about life. He realized that once hurt it is up to us to deal with it. Nothing the person who hurt him could possibly help him at this point. That is true for all of us once we are hurt.

Sure someone can give back what they stole, or they can say they are sorry, but any hurt we have is still ours to deal with no matter what.

When we accept that our partner has hurt us and start taking care of ourselves it is easier. It is easier still if we live that way all the time by anticipating times when we can take care of ourselves by planning or by accepting what is already in front of us.

"Forgiveness is the final form of love." - Reinhold Niebuhr

CHAPTER 11
KEEPING IT POSSIBLE

Everyone knows what love means! Well we all maybe do know, but whether we could agree on what it means or not is more of the question. The Greeks had a word for brotherly love that they used to describe emotional love; they had another word for erotic love, and a word for wanting good for another person. Many languages have numerous words for love, because it is so difficult to define. Hebrew has 11 words for love. There are words that are only used to express love of woman for another woman (it occurs only in the Song of Solomon in the Bible.)And others that are used only to designate the love that God has for us. I have met people so frustrated with the English word love that they refused to use it because they felt like it was overused to manipulate others, and devalued through other overuse by implying strong like of a food, or thing, as well as referring to an emotion that seems fleeting. At least the Greeks didn't have any emotional requirement on having agape love or wanting good for someone. You didn't have to feel anything to want good for others.

Creating the feeling is what this book is about and one of the important steps to being able to freely love is knowing what it means. The definition I would like to propose is wanting good for the other person. That takes a commitment, and a willingness to act accordingly to help bring about good things for the other person. However, I would propose that we speak of being in love as that emotional connection that we first talked about in the book. We can get there by first wanting good and acting upon that and the suggestions in this book. Making the choice to want good for another person and wanting to be in love with them helps, but let's take one thing at a time.

Keeping a state of being "in love" is going to be made easier by being able to forgive ourselves and our partner. If there is a word that has less agreement about what it means than love it is forgiveness. There are folks who can easily forgive and others who seem to balk at forgiving others as well as themselves. There are folks who have such rules for forgiveness that they assume everyone does that talking with them makes for difficult conversation because they assume that you think or agree with them.

When I worked at the Women's prison I dealt with forgiveness every day. Forgiveness was something that was a constant in everything that I did, and even just to be able to work there. I had lived and breathed it in every way possible that I could think of. I believed that I knew what it meant. In fact, I would have suggested that because of working with it every day that I knew more than most people.

Actually I was probably a little smug about it and believed I knew a lot about forgiveness. I had gone to great lengths to understand it and utilize it. Do you have any idea how difficult it is to help someone feel forgiven? It is something that you simply can't say you are forgiven and it has any real impact. For example, I realized that in order for me to successfully forgive people in the prison as the Chaplain I had to really become able to put myself in their shoes and recognize how I was similar and could have committed the act that brought them to prison. If I didn't emotionally go to that extreme then my words would be mostly hollow and not believed. It is no small thing to be willing to find a capacity inside you to have committed all sorts of horrible crimes. It teaches you all sorts of things about forgiveness, and about humility. The truth is all of us have that capacity but we protect ourselves from realizing it by distancing ourselves from thinking in those ways. By being willing to see those capacities inside of myself I had to grow and face some things that were not pleasant. However, by being willing to find and discover my ability to and capacity to have done the exact thing they did when I treated them with compassion it indirectly implied that they were forgiven. It was an effective tool and it impacted both of us in real ways. I learned quickly enough that just telling someone they were forgiven wasn't going to have much impact on healing someone's guilt and shame. So I learned that I needed to accept in myself what they had done and begin there. I had to find the capacity to do exactly what they had done to be really believable.

It may have been the most difficult and rewarding aspect of being the Chaplain. It meant that I had to find how I could have killed, stolen, or cheated people that were family as well as strangers. It meant discovering the similarity between me and any woman who committed the worst crime. Intellectually we all know that we are similar. However, most of us want to have a barrier between us and them, so that we could keep up the illusion that we couldn't possibly do what they did. The truth is that as a human being we all could do every conceivable crime that others have committed. It is part of our being human.

I spent years doing this and growing from the experience. I realized pretty quickly that the things I had the most difficulty forgiving were more about me than about the crime. I didn't want to forgive those similar things in my life I hadn't forgiven. In fact, that was one thing I soon discovered was the biggest block to forgiving someone of a crime was either my pride that I didn't want to be able to recognize I could have done exactly the same thing because I found the crime so disgusting, or that I hadn't forgiven myself for something similar in type if not in character. For example one woman who had spontaneously hurt her child in a bout of anger, I found myself not being able to forgive her for the longest time I couldn't figure it out. I wondered if it was because the woman was so angry still, or that her daughter who she had hurt was so young. If it had been that it would have given me relief and I would have been able to forgive her. Nothing worked, until I realized that I too had on two occasions in my youth hurt people by spontaneously doing things. Once when a friend and I were in the woods and near a small creek I found a rock and spontaneously sent it flying to splash my friend. Just as I threw the rock, my friend bent down and the rock hit him in the head. He bled as if a hose was turned on. In a matter of minutes he had blood all down his front. While it wasn't serious it was enough blood that he was freaked out. His mother didn't forgive me for that and refused for me to be around her son after that incident. It didn't matter that I apologized, or that it was an accident.

On another occasion while playing crocket, when missing a wicket that should have been an easy shot, I swung my club angrily, behind me. It hit another friend on top of his head. He had to have a couple of stitches. Neither he nor his mother ever forgave me, either to my face. Perhaps if my family hadn't moved a couple of months after these two incidents it may have turned out differently. When I remembered these two events, I had no trouble forgiving the woman, because I was then able to forgive myself.

As people we are all capable of horrible acts. It is because we are all capable of horrible acts that doing incredible good acts is worthwhile.

After about 20 or more years of examining me over every horrible crime that anyone committed that came to prison I believed that I knew a lot. I thought I knew an enormous amount about forgiveness. Besides I had realized that just because I might say to someone they were forgiven that wasn't going to help them much. They had to become able to forgive themselves as well as whom ever also hurt them. It is actually a very difficult and complicated thing to help someone forgive themselves. It often has to be done indirectly, and by implication or through a process that helps the person to recognize a whole variety of things that can and often do block their ability to forgive themselves.

So when a friend of mine caused me to read Simon Wiesenthal's book <u>Sunflowers</u> and I realized that I was only beginning to understand, it was a shock and a very real growing experience. It also let me know that others had ideas that ranged from one extreme to another. The book tells the story of what Simon Wiesenthal experienced in WWII while he was in a concentration camp. He was taken from the camp to work at a hospital and then chosen by a dying Nazi to hear the Nazi's confession of killing Jews. Since he Simon was a Jew the Nazi wanted to confess to him, and wanted him to forgive him for what he had done. The book is about whether Simon should forgive the Nazi or not. It isn't as straight forward as it might sound. The genius of the book is that beyond the first two chapters that are the story, the rest of the book is made up of distinguished theologians weighing in on the matter of whether he should forgive or not. The answers range from absolutely not to absolutely yes, and mostly everything in between. There isn't a consensus of Christians even of similar denomination let alone of various denominations. There isn't a consensus even among Jews. It was an incredibly eye opening experience for me because I realized that people see forgiveness in so many ways that I hadn't even thought of that acting as if we all know what it means isn't even reasonable.

Some folks define forgiveness as a state where we openly wipe clean the slate of what a person has done to hurt us. Others define forgiveness as something that can only be given if the right contrition is offered. Some seem to believe that by forgiving the other person we excuse it or make it acceptable what they did. I suspect it is more complicated than that.

When I speak of forgiveness it means something quite specific. For me forgiveness means that I am letting go of my right to seek revenge for what you have done to me. I am no longer going to have to carry around the hurt that you did to me by your actions. Now your actions are entirely between you and God. I have no right to forgive your actions that have been sinful. That is between you and God. I can also choose to forgive whether you say or do anything to make it right because my being able to forgive you doesn't depend on you. If forgiving depended upon the person who hurt us then any cruel thing a person could do to us would then give them power over us until they chose to be contrite. That wouldn't be fair, and it wouldn't square with how things are. We get the right to forgive no matter what. It doesn't mean their behavior has been excused. It doesn't mean they are off the hook. The hook is now between them and God. There are always consequences, and there is nothing I can do about those even if I wanted to, because it has nothing to do with rules or laws it is the consequences of our actions.

Another thing that I learned at the prison was that there is no such thing as getting away with anything. Oh, sure people commit crimes and don't get caught, but no one gets away with anything. From the biggest to the smallest thing that we do there are consequences. It doesn't mean that everyone will be able to see them but there are consequences for everything that we do. There are good consequences and bad ones. No, I am not talking about karma but the fact that anything we do impacts us as well.

How come all this talk about forgiveness, you might ask. It is because forgiveness is a large part of what makes being able to be loving possible. If we haven't been forgiving others we won't be able to feel forgiven ourselves. If we think that their sins are worse than ours it is only a matter of time till life would give us a corrective emotional experience where we would have the opportunity to learn how near sighted that attitude is. However, when a person forgives they have the freedom to feel good about themselves. They can also learn to forgive themselves. It may be one of the most difficult concepts that any of us learn, and it is in the words of the Lord's Prayer. Forgive us as we forgive others, is the idea. Forgive us our debts as we forgive our debtors, is the way it is often translated. Some Churches say forgive us our trespasses as we forgive those who trespass against us. The idea is the same. We are encouraged to forgive as we want to be forgiven. What we are seldom taught is that is also the way it works. We get to feel and live as forgiven as we have forgiven. (By the way, this prayer called the Lord's Prayer is actually two standard Jewish prayers that Jesus put together and isn't original to him. Folks have been saying things like that for a very long time before Jesus came along.

It may be one of the single most powerful ways of helping ourselves to heal from any hurt from the past. The way it works in almost every situation is a bit odd and won't seem straight forward. I am going to tell a story about a young woman who I knew at the prison to illustrate how it works.

Deanna was a young woman who was very unpleasant to be around. She would splash her anger toward others and if it wasn't her anger it was her sexuality. She was attractive and she would dress, sit, stand and look sexually appealing. It wasn't something that she did consciously, but it was certainly a part of how she related to others. It didn't matter whether they were male or female. Deanna was seductive toward them, or around them. She however didn't really know she was seductive toward anyone.

Deanna had been sexually abused as a child and she had been to therapy. She believed that she was fine. She was in trouble for some minor rule violation but she knew that something wasn't right. She wanted to change. She knew that everyone wasn't as angry or as prone to getting into trouble.

I suspected that she had hidden the shame and disbeliefs she had about herself when she had been in counseling earlier. I believed that she was blaming herself secretly and wasn't likely to acknowledge it. So I said to her the following.

"Deanna, I want to talk with you and say some things that perhaps your earlier therapist didn't say. You don't need to respond to what I am saying. It is important enough for us to simply acknowledge that I have said these things to you. One of the things that seems to plague people who were sexually abused is that they secretly identify with the perpetrator and when people tell them how wrong the perpetrator was they will agree with them but they will feel condemned. There are several reasons that people have difficulty forgiving themselves and one of the reasons is that they have told themselves that because their body responded they believed they were wrong. They saw themselves like the perpetrator, and therefore experienced any blame to the perpetrator as blame of them.

I went on, "There are other reasons a person who has been abused is likely to blame her/himself that are connected to the abuse. In the first place a child who has a secret with an adult will feel very separated and alone from all other people. They will feel close to the perpetrator and not realize it was because of sharing a secret. It is pseudo-closeness. It is a closeness that isn't real but would feel real. People who have been in those relationships and haven't known how to cope with their feeling drawn toward people who hurt them in similar ways that the first person did. When they realize the hurt and shame they encountered in the past impacted them in powerful ways, then they can forgive but they have to forgive themselves first. I know you probably thought I was going to say the person who abused you, but you first have to forgive yourself partially for your body responding and for being normal so that your body did respond. You know it is as simple as that if we put tight shoes on you and walked you around the block it is likely that you would get blisters, because that is what happens when a person's body is rubbed in those ways. If a person's body was rubbed in other ways it would cause a response as well. It simply means you are normal. Now after you forgive yourself some you may want to forgive the person who abused you. Forgiving them simply frees you. It doesn't take away from what they did. We can help you heal, but knowing that you can forgive him is a good thing, because you want to feel forgiven as well."

She changed. She became a different person. She stopped being seductive and stopped being on the verge of being in trouble. She had more patience. She had more hope and was able to tolerate a lot of different people. She became a model prisoner.

Because I was accepting of her and addressing some of the things that occurred that she kept using to ratify her negative beliefs about herself. She was very changed person. In fact, she was able to forgive the person who hurt her as well. She became a model inmate. She became a changed person overnight.

I could tell lots of those types of stories. They would always end with how changed the person became as they were able to forgive themselves and forgive the people who had harmed them. Often you would see such a beauty in folks who have managed to forgive in spite of a great loss. It is as if it blessed them in powerful and amazing ways. Those folks may just have realized that forgiveness is for you, not for the other person. Your forgiving someone frees you. It doesn't free them.

The need to be right is the sign of a vulgar mind.
- Albert Camus

CHAPTER 12
THE OTHER SIDE OF FORGIVENESS

The stories about folks who couldn't or wouldn't forgive others are not so pleasant. They are of people who are determined to be right no matter what. They know they were hurt and are not forgiving because they don't have to, don't want to and are certain they are right. For example one woman who wouldn't forgive her mother for the transgressions her mother had committed 20 years earlier lost two jobs because the anger she had about her mother simply slopped out of her where ever she went. Until she lost the second job she didn't even believe that her anger impacted her at all.

Actually, I know stories about people who made their lives miserable because of not forgiving someone else who had hurt them. Their anger festered and stole much from them but they didn't want to acknowledge that once hurt it was theirs to fix.

While I know that in some circles it is not politically correct to say it is in our best interest to forgive but I have never seen the opposite work well. I do believe that the folks who are saying it isn't necessary to forgive are people who have a concept of forgiveness that exonerates the aggressor. Forgiveness is for the person who has been hurt. It won't really fix the problems of the one who did the hurting. No matter how much you forgive me, I still have to forgive myself and deal with my image of God in forgiving me as well. I have never seen anyone who refused to forgive not pay a high price for their unwillingness to forgive. I have seen people who swore they didn't pay any price and refused to believe their anger had any effect on anyone else, and certainly not on themselves. I guess it was or is just too close to home.

In fact, on numerous occasions I have seen a person who was hurt and holding anger toward the person who hurt them has some incredible epiphanies. It would generally be that the person who hurt them would appear totally untroubled by what they had done. In fact, the perpetrator even seemed to blame the person they hurt for being hurt. Denial seems to work that way. One woman in prison was angry at the woman who died during the holdup she had participated in. When asked how come she was angry at the woman who was killed, she said, "If she hadn't been so tall she wouldn't have been killed." I couldn't make something like that up. It is the sort of thing that people say to justify their wrongs. They have to heal enough to become able to even see how distorted they have become in order to heal more.

Ironically once the victim actually healed enough to forgive the perpetrator then somehow almost as if a switch were thrown the perpetrator began to feel guilt for what they had done. How the perpetrator knew, I don't know. How it had any effect, I don't know. All I am telling you is what I have observed. It may have to do with mirroring neurons in that when I forgive you and am no longer holding anger toward you for what you did to me, that you then have to cope with your own feelings instead of the anger I had toward you. Often when someone is angry with us we either are totally indifferent or it bothers us a lot. Somehow forgiving the perpetrator set in motion the set of actions that made the perpetrator have to deal with their own actions.

Even if you don't believe me that this is part of what happens because you can't see any way that it would, you could believe it if God was involved. You could easily believe that God would nudge the person more who was wrong when the victim of their abuse had forgiven them. Even if it isn't a good reason to forgive someone in order that they have to feel their own shame and remorse, it certainly helps when we know that in order to get better the person will have to admit their responsibility.

In testing this out when two people hurt me I decided to forgive them. I prayed about being able to forgive them and let it go putting the entire responsibility in God's hands. Ok, well I had to do it a number of times but it was made easier because I know that anyone doing things as nasty as what they did to me will reap consequences that would be far more powerful than any revenge I could affix. So it wasn't because of my being so saintly that I could forgive but because I know that carrying it hurts me and that ultimately there is no such thing as getting away with anything. But this time I got an even better surprise. Something even better happened.

The one who I saw regularly acted very differently after I forgave her. No one knew except for God and me that I had forgiven them. No one was told and there was absolutely no way either of them could have known. However, the next time I saw her she couldn't look me in the eye. My forgiving them had not only freed me but had put something on them. I saw both of them again several times and each time although it was very awkward for them to not look at me they managed it. The other people with them must have sensed how awkward it was, and it also must have been doubly awkward since I too knew the other people, who all spoke to me and treated me with respect. Overall it was very satisfying and gratifying. It was better than just some positive emotional experience. It gave me a truth. One person's forgiveness can impact another person in powerful ways. I have since seen it occur a number of times. It is the most rewarding experience because it acknowledges all sorts of spiritual things by its occurring.

Being forgiven for committing acts of aggression doesn't fix the problem for the person who committed the offense. A story that plagued me demonstrates this I think well. A mother came to prison for maiming her child in a fit of anger. The child was the most accepting, loving and forgiving person you could ever want to meet. The child had forgiven her mother. If anything that made it more difficult for the mom. The mother wouldn't even hear of forgiving herself. She was making sure that she paid way above what the court imposed on her. She was harsh on herself for her act and there was nothing that was going to change it.

Prisons are supposed to be filled with people who all claim they are innocent. That wasn't my experience. What I saw was people who accepted readily what they had done and mostly blamed themselves for it. It was actually rare for women at the prison to claim innocence. Some of the ones who claimed it actually were or at least they were treated that way by the court. Actually, the only people who were consistently in denial about their involvement in crime were people who had committed sexual crimes against children.

However, it was common in prison that a person was harboring anger toward someone just like everywhere else. There are people who are angry and who refuse to forgive. Sometimes they are just scared and don't know how to forgive because they feel vulnerable. Sometimes it is people who are simply angry and defiant. They have no willingness to forgive. Those folks are a different sort. They are angry and hurt and they have no intention of forgiving because they have been hurt and they want either revenge, or they want some sigh that clearly shows their willingness to be contrite. Folks who are not willing to forgive can be quite pleasant in other ways but they still suffer from their perspective that sets them up.

Recently, I started to see a refusal to forgive as a spiritual state that isn't likely to get fixed easily. It tends to be people who don't seem like they know a very loving God. Or else they have had such a negative experience that was accentuated by the person hurting them seeming to get away with murder. That we can't always see the cost someone else pays doesn't detract from the price they pay. Unfortunately, carrying anger means a person is more likely to do other things that are not good for themselves or for others. While being angry and refusing to forgive others may not always be a sign of a spiritual problem it can point in that direction.

It makes the person refusing to forgive to be treating themselves like God. They are refusing to forgive even though they want to be forgiven. It isn't an easy place to impact because the person who refuses doesn't see anything wrong with their position. They feel either totally justified because of how angry they are or they are indifferent. Either way they are sentencing themselves to the repercussions of not forgiving. Not only does that sort of judgmental attitude hurt people but it leads to even more unfortunate consequences. For instance, it leads later to feeling condemned by our own judgmental stance that we took toward someone else. Either we or one of our families will bring this realization to us in a big way. Folks who need to hear this won't read it or if they do it won't mean anything to them. You who already know the truth of it can affirm it but you already know it.

True love begins when nothing is looked for in return."
—Antoine De Saint-Exupery

CHAPTER 13
TRANSFORMING DISAGREEMENTS EASILY

The book started off inviting you to a positive place by remembering positive times when you were in love. One of the ways we can get to that place is by remembering those types of times. If you want to review that chapter right now you will see that all I did was invite you to remember some obvious truths about your being in love and how it felt and what occurred to you as a result. There are other ways but for now let's begin to deal with disagreements, from a positive place.

Most disagreements that occur are not even a real disagreement at all. If you check what each of you mean by a word or phrase it will become obvious. Webster's unabridged dictionary has very few words that have only one meaning. Usually those words are technical and new. All the rest of the words in the dictionary have more than one meaning and many have meanings that are seemed almost opposites. Take the word manipulate. The first meaning in the dictionary is not the one that you probably first thought of or do think of when you hear the word manipulate. The first definition is of effective handling. The second meaning is about the covert control that is being used, and is probably the one you first thought of. Two people can argue about the meaning of manipulation and both are exactly right. There are lots of words that are like that and when you consider the larger picture that there are also regional differences in what words mean you have an even larger problem. I have a dictionary of words that have different meanings based upon regions. It is actually quite large, and has taught me quite a lot, about language.

So if we begin with the understanding that both of you can be right and probably are then we can deal with the disagreement in a positive manner. In fact, it can become a means to the two of you getting closer. Intimacy is about learning and being shown the uniqueness of your partner in a way that helps the two of you feel closer. What better way than to utilize disagreements to assist you to become closer. When you discover how come the two of you see a word, phrase or meaning of something differently it is very likely to draw you closer.

Even disagreements about things that can or can not be easily solved because there is not right or wrong answer can be dealt with from a positive trance where we are aware of all our strengths. One disagreement that my wife and I had was about the fruit called a paw paw. It is typical in that the reasons for us both being so passionate about our answer has to do with something we normally don't pay a lot of attention to, because we would have felt so threatened. She pointed to what she knew to be a paw paw and it wasn't what I had been taught was one. Since, both of us had been taught about Paw Paws by our grandmothers it was an issue of loyalty. We both wanted to be loyal and be seen as loyal to our grandmothers. If you asked us both about when we learned about paw paws you would also get warm memories of closeness that we shared with our grandmothers. The right answer wasn't what was but the meaning behind what we shared with someone who was important to us.

That same type of argument occurred about chili, and there is no way of resolving it with a picture in the dictionary. For my wife chili involves spaghetti, and a pinch of sugar, along with the usual ingredients. Where I grew up and in my family of origin chili never saw spaghetti, and sugar was never added to meat. Again if you ask us how come this is important to us it has to do with loyalty to what we knew as children. Of course there is no real right answer about chili, (well I still think there is) but getting to know how come it is important to each of us also was a means of getting closer. It isn't just the regional and familial differences of ingredients about chili. My father was the one in my family who made chili. My liking it the way he made it is about the warm memories I have of his always being loving and accepting of me as a person. He always believed in me. Since, my mother died when I was young and I was an only child, he and I were very close. Since he too is no longer here, eating chili the way he made it is an act of nostalgia for me that has warm memories. No matter what we are both right about chili.

I so frequently told one couple that they were both right that when they would begin to disagree they would compete about who said the phrase first that they were both right. They would laugh and then begin to discover how they were both right. They have a great relationship now and are fun to be around, because they now use any disagreement to allow them to become closer. Until they learned this approach they were often caught up in the customary way of understanding disagreements that our culture suggests. They are both bright and recognized how useful this approach is. It has worked because the last time I saw them in the community they were almost bubbling with love for each other. You might have thought they were teenagers in love.

Often disagreements occur because one of the couple is in a negative trance, and not seeing things as completely as they could. We all get into negative trances from time to time because of fear, anger, hurt, sadness, or even joy, euphoria and excitement. Our tunnel vision of focusing on one subject is the issue because the narrowing of what we are options and possibilities makes talking with us difficult. Sometimes all it takes is the right nudge and the negative trance is broken and then there is no argument.

One couple that I was seeing illustrates this well. The man was trying to tell his wife that he loved her so much that he wanted to eliminate the disagreement they had by doing something different. He was going to go out of his way just so that there wouldn't be an argument. What she heard was that he wanted a divorce. The man said it again in a different way and again his wife heard him saying that he wanted to be away from her and wanted a divorce. She didn't want to give him one but would as there wasn't anything to do but that. I tried to fix the miscommunication and failed miserably. It wasn't making any sense. Her husband was saying he loved her so much that he was willing to go out of his way to show that and what she was hearing was that he wanted a divorce. I was getting frustrated and I could tell the woman was about to get up and walk out of my office, when suddenly the disagreement was ended by a sudden good fortune.

My lab that accompanies me seeing people got up off the floor where she was laying and went over and put her nose in the woman's lap. Suddenly, the woman exclaimed, "Oh, I get it you really do love me", and then looked so lovingly at her husband that it would have melted your heart. The woman's negative trance was broken in the moment the dog touched her. The loving act of the dog sensing her hurt was all it took to break the spell that held her from seeing what was right in front of her and obvious. Unfortunately, or fortunately it is always obvious when we can see it from a different perspective and until we do we usually think there is no other way to see things than the way we are seeing. From the woman's perspective she was only able to hear what she heard.

A while back while driving on the highway and thinking about Catholic Sisters I saw a billboard in the distance, and was surprised to see that the ad featured a young Catholic Sister. I smiled and was very pleased to see it, until as I got closer and realized my imagination had played a trick on me. It wasn't a Catholic Sister that I wanted to be on the Billboard but a young woman with her hair in a towel. She wasn't a Sister in a habit. The dark around her that I assumed to be the dark of a Catholic Sister's outfit was the woman's dark hair. What we are thinking of and what we are afraid of seeing can distort what we perceive.

If you think that distortions are not the norm, then you haven't been to a family reunion recently. Because if you had been you would have had the experience of people remembering things you didn't and vice versa. It isn't that only one is correct, it may be that both of you are correct. It may also be that both of you remember a distortion based upon what you wanted to remember.

Neuroscience is clear that our remembering is based upon what is needed to be remembered rather than some digital recording. Our culture has implied that our memory is like recordings and it simply isn't. (Well, except for the few people who have the condition where they cannot forget or not remember everything that happened to them.) It is actually a terrible condition that is unpleasant. Imagine not being able to forget those terrible long moments, or unpleasant pains, events, or.......

Beginning from or even beginning again from a positive place is simply accepting that the fluid nature of communication and perception are a fact of life and allowing that to be a humorous occasion, or at least a teaching one.

You probably have times when you have seen, heard, or believed something that simply wasn't when you checked again later. I remember the porch on the house I grew up in as huge. It was very tall and went across the front and side of the house. As an adult when I went back to that same house and I was shocked to realize the porch was only about 3 feet off the ground. I had remembered it as 6 or 7 feet high. Beginning from a positive trance is simply accepting that type of distortion to memory and continuing on, perhaps with a smile and perhaps with a question mark in our mind.

You may only be one person to the world, but you may also be the world to one person." - Anonymous quote

CHAPTER 14
WAYS OF GENERATING A POSITIVE MINDSET

Of course you can generate a positive trance by remembering a time when you were in one. You can focus on that time and allow yourself to go there in as deep of a way as you can. Simply remembering in an intentional way with more than one of the senses operating can be a powerful experience. For example, when you remember the songs that you listened to when you first met and fell in love and think about any scene of you two being together it would be a stronger and deeper trance of remembering that you could utilize.

If there was a smell associated with you two being together such as a favorite perfume, a smell of honeysuckle, or fresh cut grass that was/is a sensory key to remembering it can make it even more powerful.

You can remember any other time that you felt powerfully alive and with that sense of ability and strength that seems so wonderful. It can become a springboard. Any time that you felt that powerful ability and awareness of everything around you would work for our purposes, because the positive trance is a positive trance it doesn't have to be only when you two were in love, a positive trance can come from any of those times when you felt really alive. You might allow yourself to go to one of those places right now. It feels pretty good does it not? I bet that if you are able to be in that positive place of a positive trance where you are aware of yourself, your strengths, and your surroundings and you are also aware of how good you feel then you have achieved the state we were looking for.

Sometimes people use music, places, foods, or textures of things to help them achieve that state. At different times people refer to this state of mind as a whole range of things. You might call it flow, being present in the now, being fully aware, or just a state of heightened awareness. Whatever you call it most all of us have experienced times like it. You may have been in that time when you were answering questions on a text, or batting when no one expected you to even get on base and you hit a home run. It could have been when you were playing tennis, swimming, driving, or doing anything that you enjoy, because you felt alive.

Another way to achieve that state of being highly aware takes a little practice but since you have been thinking about it by reading the above you may well be able to do it right now. The approach is simple. All you have to do is keep your head and eyes looking forward and allow yourself to become aware of everything around you in the room. It doesn't have to be from your peripheral vision, just allow yourself to become aware of and sense things around you right now where you are right now. Now increase your intensity and allow yourself to be aware of things even further from you, and at the same time notice the calm in your body and the confidence you can have as you take a deep breath. As you let the air out appreciate how pleasant you are beginning to feel, even while you realize that you also are aware of the things around you and yourself at the same time, while you also are noticing the pleasantness and comfort that is there in your body.

Some people get so that they can think about being in this state of calm and achieve it by simply taking a deep breath and remembering that you can achieve that state of hyper awareness easily enough any time you would like to. All you really have to do is to want to go there and perhaps shift your current focus enough so that you can go into a positive trance. I know people who can do this very quickly now that they have learned that they can.

Because it is simply utilizing a normal state of mind that we often go into it can become something you can use easily. You may not be as quick to use this state intentionally but you can experience it as almost magical. In a sense it is because when replacing a negative trance with this positive one you will regain your ability to see more clearly and with more of the options that you were born with and that our culture and fear stole from you. It helps you to see and recognize what your strengths are. In this place you are less defensive, and more confident as well as calm and assured.

What is even better is that this feeling and emotional state can help you become even better at whatever you do, allowing the fear to become less and your strength, awareness and being fully present to become more.

If for some reason none of the above means seem to work for you at this point then we may need to do something different. It simply is something that you can do very intentionally. You would notice your fear, or your block to achieving what state you want and see it on a TV screen, with a little indention in the screen of another scene. The second scene would be small and in the corner of the first screen.

That smaller screen would be a time when you were powerful, aware and fully present. Allow the big screen to become smaller and the smaller screen to become larger until they trade places. Repeat the exercise several times, and now allow yourself to be in the scene of the powerful time.

If you are not someone who easily visualizes scenes then do the same thing with a feeling. Allow the feeling of being overwhelmed and defeated to be something you are aware of or what ever feeling seems to be blocking you and then allow yourself the smallest awareness of the times when you are powerful and aware to be there with you even if it is only in a very small amount. Allow the two to switch several times until you can notice the feeling changing and your awareness changing with it.

The man who taught me the technique likes me a lot. He is a very deliberate and thoughtful man. I value his friendship. You can value your own connections to any ways that help you to achieve a positive state of mind.

Another way that some find the most successful in helping them to achieve a positive place is to accept anywhere and any feeling that you are having right now, and then begin adding to it awareness of touch, sounds, sights, and smells that you can also become aware of. As you continue to add experiences and awareness into the picture the feeling that you were having and wanting to replace has occurred because the gradual adding into awareness of everything else alters our conscious mental state powerfully. Sometimes that is all it takes to shift from a negative trance to a positive one. Knowing that the expansion of your awareness alters your way of thinking is pretty amazing. The better you get at this the better it becomes a positive tool for you.

Often the texture of touch is a surprising one to most folks because it is one that we don't spend a lot of time with. So adding the texture of something around you by touching it and then adding in other sensory events so that you can walk your way to a better place where your focus shifts so that you can be both focused and connected to a positive place as well as aware of everything around you.

"Love is the master key that opens the gates of happiness."
- Oliver Wendell Holmes

CHAPTER 15
COPING WITH YOUR NEW LOVE PROSPERITY

Some folks will sense that your relationship is positive and they may be curious about how it is that you achieved such a state of being in love that they noticed it. Of course some will be putting themselves down in your presence and being just jealous, instead of being inspired. It is too bad because it is easier to achieve from a state of being inspired instead of jealous. I like to think of it as a positive thing and one that can allow others to realize they too can achieve a state of being in love. If someone seems truly determined to put themselves down in your presence you can share the book with them. Or if you see someone who really is almost there you can share the book with them and see how quickly they too can achieve a state of being in love.

I like to also think of this state as being one that affirms our faith in a powerful way, because it is utilizing many of the same tools to achieve a more powerful and satisfying relationship that we get to be in with our partner and with God.

When people see the genuine intimacy between you and your partner some may not believe it. Others if you tell them how you are doing it might just scoff and criticize you and the approach, because this is going to a place few other couples go. As I said in the beginning of the book there are people who don't believe this is possible. They think that people have to argue to be in a good relationship. They really don't realize that arguing isn't necessary and that remaining in love is something very possible and certainly do able.

Skeptics love to discuss how the divorce rate is so high. They also don't mention that of people who regularly attend church or synagogue it is much lower. The numbers for the general public is 1 in 2 marriages fail. The number of marriages that fail of people who attend regular worship services is only 1 in 10. There is a reason for that, and it isn't just that believers stay in unhappy marriages. It is that the Bible gives us ways that help us to be able to stay in a relationship. It is also that faith and our relationship with God brings us blessings that easily translate into stability and longevity of life and marriage. It is likely that a lot of things all coming together are what make the difference for the believer. Yes it probably is that believers tend to take their commitments more seriously. Yes it probably is also that there would be more of a social upheaval for the believer to divorce and so they find ways of making it work. There are probably lots of reasons that contribute to regular worship attendees having a lower divorce rate. If because there are social pressures for a person to find other ways to solve their relational problems with their partner than to divorce then that can be a good thing. It means that giving people more tools helps them make better decisions. If staying together is an option then they can look for other ways of doing that. Actually, people interviewed 5 years after a divorce and five years after attending counseling and staying married gave a very startling answer. The majority of people who stayed married and worked it out were happier.

Please don't think that I am saying all relationships are salvageable. They are not. Divorce is a necessary and useful tool that helps people get out of relationships that are terrible and unlikely to get better. What I am saying is that with a good relationship there are things that can be done to help it and bring about positive change.

Getting accustomed to others looking up to you may be something that is coming. As such one of the most powerful ways is to be humble about it and give the credit to your faith, and spouse. Just letting yourself be complimented or even teased for achieving something that others tend not to is difficult. Letting yourself be an inspiration for others is probably even more difficult. Let's admit that what you have done to get here is a big deal. You let yourself recognize that you single-handedly could make a difference in how you felt in your marriage. You went against the grain of our culture and recognized that things you were not happy with your spouse about spoke first and foremost about you, and you took steps to improve those things. Finally you began to treat your spouse's words, actions and even tones as if they really loved you, while you continued to do loving things that suggested your commitment. That took no small commitment and made a huge difference in how you felt and how your partner treated you. Along the way you may also have improved your relationship with God. So when people praise you or are astounded that you and your partner get along so well and are close, take the compliment. You both made changes because I guarantee that because of the changes you made your partner made many as well.

Happiness is generally considered transitory and dependent upon events that we often have little control over. Yet real happiness tends to come from our ability to bring value to the world in one way or another, about things that have meaning to us. It is very probable that you are much happier, and more content because of your willingness to take care of yourself and your future through altering how you interact with your partner.

ABOUT THE AUTHOR

Dr Lentz is the Director of the Ericksonian Institute of Jeffersonville, Indiana; where he teaches and practices hypnosis as well as Marriage and Family Therapy. He is also the minister at Radcliff Presbyterian Church where his sermons are as intentionally hypnotic and healing as he can craft them. You can request the sermons to be delivered to your email by asking. They currently go to many places around the country and internationally. He lives with his wife in the log cabin they built together soon after they were married.

He is the Author of the following books.
Double Binds: The DNA of Emotional and Mental Problems and How to Make use of Their Positive Potential,
Trance Altering: Epiphanies You can Create,
Transforming Mis-Communication,
Compassionate Healing of Sex Addicts and the People Who Love Them,
How the Word Heals: Hypnosis in Scriptures,
Spiritual Solutions to Anxiety and Panic Disorder,

Effective Handling of Manipulative Persons.
Therapeutic Meditations: 40 Days and 40 Nights to Change

The next three books he is working on include the topics of Healing Bi-Polar Conversations, Healing and Dealing with Borderline Personality Disorder, and The Alchemy of Emotions: New Options and New Possibilities.

He is a member of or also holds supervisory status with the American Association of Marriage and Family Therapy, The American Association of Pastoral Counselors, The American Society of Clinical Hypnosis, and the International Society of Clinical Hypnosis.

He is a popular speaker about a variety of subjects both nationally and internationally. Some of the subject he has addressed recently have been the following. How to Stay in Love Forever, Enhancing Immunity, From Panic to Peace, An Ericksonian Approach to Panic Disorder, Manipulation and Miscommunication, New Approaches to Healing Trauma, Compassionate Healing of Sex Addicts, From Trauma to Triumph, Innovative Treatment of Borderline Personality Disorder, Protecting Yourself From Toxic Emotions: While Positively helping others at the same time, and Healing Bi-Polar Disorder. He has a variety of Hypnosis CD's also available that deal with subjects such as self esteem, sleep, criticism, addiction, procrastination, loneliness, anger, forgiveness and effective test taking. He can be reached for arranging workshops or for having sermons sent each week to you at Lentshome@aol.com

www.ingramcontent.com/pod-product-compliance
Lightning Source LLC
Chambersburg PA
CBHW060158050426
42446CB00013B/2895